BLESS 'EM ALL

BLESS 'EM ALL

THE LANES OF CORK

EIBHLÍS DE BARRA

MERCIER PRESS

MERCIER PRESS
PO Box 5, 5 French Church Street, Cork
and
16 Hume Street, Dublin

Trade enquiries to CMD DISTRIBUTION,
55a Spruce Avenue, Stillorgan Industrial Park, Blackrock, Dublin

© Eibhlís de Barra 1997

ISBN 1 85635 175 0

10 9 8 7 6 5 4 3 2

A CIP record for this book is available from the British Library.

ACKNOWLEDGEMENT

I wish to acknowledge my sincerest thanks to Pádraig Tyers without whose
help this book would never have seen the light of day. It was he who first
suggested that I write it. Ever since then he has given unstintingly of his
time and advice and made my task easier than it would have otherwise been.

Printed in Ireland by Colour Books Ltd.

CONTENTS

True Corkonian

It has always been said that to qualify as a true Corkonian one must be able to boast of at least one city-born grandmother. I can justifiably lay claim to that distinction as both my grandmothers were natives of Cork. My mother's mother, Elizabeth Duggan, was born in Broad Lane which ran from Grattan Street to the North Main Street but has long since disappeared. As a young girl she caught the eye of a boy named John Kingston, a publican's son from Clonakilty, who was apprenticed to the bootmaking trade at Croft's in the North Main Street. During his apprenticeship there he lived on the premises and shortly after he had served his time he and Elizabeth got married. He set up in business in a small shop in Gilabbey Street but later moved up a few doors to No. 13 at the corner of Ninety Eight Street. That was a larger premises with ample living accommodation overhead. John and Elizabeth had eight children, six of whom survived, and my mother Madge was middleways in the family.

In due course Madge met a young man named Geoffrey McCarthy, and after a few years' courtship they decided to tie the knot. However the wedding had to be postponed for a while due to the fact that shortly before the appointed date my Aunt Jane's husband was involved in a fatal accident on his way to work at the Franciscan Well Mineral Water Company premises on the North Mall. As he stepped off a bus a part of his clothing got caught in the door and he was dragged under the wheel and killed. The wedding took place later on a Sunday.

Girls in those days were loath to move away from their parents' homes even on marrying, and so it was not surprising that Geoffrey and Madge settled down to their new life in two vacant rooms at the top of No. 13. It was in one of those rooms that I arrived in the land of the living, the second of a family of seven. After about ten years Mam and Dad reluctantly decided to move out. Granda and Gran were getting old and Mam felt that having five boisterous young children racing up and down stairs all day didn't allow for any great peace or quiet for an elderly couple who however had never complained. Mam and Dad also realised full well that if they remained on where they were there was no hope of ever being considered for a house by the Corporation. For these reasons and also in order to be somewhat more independent they both decided that they should move elsewhere. Their primary concern was to get accommodation somewhere close to Granda and Gran, a task which proved difficult as any accommodation available near-by was in poor condition. After a lengthy and fruitless search they finally decided to rent rooms in one of the large four-storey houses in Queen's Place beside the South Channel of the river Lee just above Clarke's Bridge. These were amongst the oldest houses in Cork and were originally inhabited by the aristocracy and merchant princes of the city, as the big iron gates leading into the area testified. It is said that the queen in question was the much-maligned Queen Caroline. Some years ago the houses were demolished to make way for the new Unemployment Exchange.

The rooms which my mother acquired were in No. 2. Having paid the landlord a month's rent in advance she proceeded to clean the rooms from top to bottom, an operation that badly needed to be done. That same operation was brought to an abrupt halt, however, when she noticed bugs in the old timber. Rats and mice she could tolerate but not creepy-crawlies, so as soon as the bugs made their appearance she dropped every-thing, ran for dear life and never looked back. She even for-feited the month's rent which cannot have been easy for her.

We continued to live in Granda's house until one day a friend of Mam's informed her that she had a house to rent at four shillings a week in Gunpowder Lane and she would give her first choice. Admittedly the house was in poor condition but we desperately needed a place of our own, and the fact that Gunpowder Lane, later renamed St Finbarr's Avenue, was within a hundred yards of Granda's appealed to Mam. Before we moved there another woman said to her: 'If I were you, Madge, I wouldn't dream of living in that house.'

'Why?' said Mam.

'Because,' she said, 'it is a very unlucky house. The woman who was living there had her husband committed to the Mental Hospital, and the woman before her again buried her husband while she was living there.'

Mam just smiled and assured her that she wasn't even remotely superstitious. It was public knowledge at the time that Gunpowder Lane and the surrounding lanes had been declared a clearance area and that the houses there would be demolished as soon as alternative housing could be provided for the inhabitants. Being resident there offered us the best chance of finally getting a new house of our own from the Corporation. Our minds were made up and so we moved to No. 17 Gunpowder Lane. The year was 1939, shortly before the outbreak of war.

I never heard the lane referred to as a anything but Gunpowder Lane but people say that that was not its original name. Seemingly some time in the last century men who lived there worked in the gunpowder factory in Ballincollig, walking out and back every day. The popular belief was that they regularly stole gunpowder, brought it home hidden under their clothes and sold it to quarry owners around Cork for blasting purposes. One night some of them gathered in a house in the lane to dry over a candle some powder which had become damp, but a serious explosion occurred resulting in the deaths of a number of unfortunate men, women and children and the destruction not only of that particular house but of other houses also. Hence the name Gunpowder Lane. That, it seems, was also the reason that there were some cowlucks in the lane. It isn't so long ago since I learned that the word 'cow-luck,' which was a very common word amongst the people of the lanes of Cork, came from the Irish word *cabhlach* meaning a ruin or roofless walls.

Our house was two-sided, which meant that the front door was in the middle with a window on either side. The accommodation consisted of two bedrooms, a kitchen, a scullery and a loft. The front door was in actual fact a full door with a half-door outside it. The half-door was a great novelty for us children but it was also very practical. The house was extremely dark inside but when the weather was suitable you could open the full door to let the light in, and yet the half-door offered a certain amount of privacy. If a woman wished to take a break from her daily chores she stood inside the half-door, rested her elbows on top of it and watched the neighbours, the odd stranger or horse or donkey go by. She was monarch of all she surveyed. While she was enjoying her balm at the door she could carry on a conversation with her neighbours, at the same time keeping an eye on her children to ensure that they weren't up to any wrongdoing, and equally important that no other children were fighting or interfering with them. If a fight did occur the mothers might scream and shout at one another. 'Let me at her, hold me back or I'll reef her to the ground!' was their favourite battle-cry. That cry might be followed by another: 'Let me at her. Hold me back!' Then the peacemaker came on the scene and the would-be combatants were restrained, as indeed they knew full well they would be.

The two bedrooms were to one side of the house, one behind the other, and the kitchen with the scullery behind it was on the other side. As the scullery was windowless we used it as a store-room. There was no gas supply in the lane so like all the other families there we had to do the cooking on an open fire. There were two hobs, one on either side of the fire, to cook meat, vegetables and anything else that needed to be boiled. If Mam wished to bake a cake or roast a kipper or a herring to which Dad was very partial she used the grid-iron which was a rectangular rack made of light iron bars and which when placed over the fire stretched across from hob to hob and acted as the equivalent of the grill of a modern cooker. There were no tiles on the fireplace, just a wooden surround, and driven into this surround at the side of the fire was a nail on which hung the button-hook, a simple yet very effective device used to close the rows of buttons which were a common feature of women's and children's footwear in those days. High up across the fireplace was a line to dry the men's socks. There was another line across the length of the ceiling for airing clothes. On the mantelpiece Mam put her 'purties', a crinoline lady, a china dog and whatever else she possessed. The fender was of steel and bore the words 'Home Sweet Home' across it. Sandpaper was used to make it gleam whereas a brass fender needed only a rub of Brasso to give it a grand shine.

The interior of the house was extremely dark. The oil-lamp in the kitchen had a double wick which in those days was considered quite a cut above the single wick. The lamp was about three feet high, with a brass stand, a paraffin bowl made of pink china and a glass globe. The two wicks had to be trimmed regularly with scissors, otherwise they smoked and dirtied the globe. The white tissue paper which came in shoe-boxes was ideal for cleaning smoky globes and was always carefully put aside for that purpose. The lamp wasn't the only thing that smoked, however. Because the open fire was always lighting the chimney regularly became clogged with soot but the sweep cost money and so our method of cleaning the chimney was the simple one of getting an old roll of wallpaper, pouring a good dousing of paraffin on it, setting it alight and pushing it up the chimney. As soon as you heard the roar of the burning paper you ran out into the lane to see the sparks and the smoke going skywards.

Inside the window that looked out on the lane Mam had her sewing-machine. For a number of years prior to our leaving Gran's house she had been taking on sewing-work from women in the area and the machine had enabled her to earn some badly needed extra money, and would continue to do so for many years to come. The kitchen tabletop was made of four white deal boards not too closely fitted together and cleaning it was best accomplished with the aid of a scrubbing brush and

11

a lump of black Sambo soap.

On winter nights we detested being ordered to bed because it meant leaving the cosy fire and facing into the freezing bedroom. Needless to say there was then no heating of the kind available nowadays. Maybe it was our imagination playing tricks on us but it did seem that those winters were extremely cold. The best we could do was to heat the clothes-iron, wrap it up in an old cardigan, put it into the bed and then we all snuggled into one another. We were young and could fit in one bed, girls at the top and boys at the bottom.

We weren't long resident in the lane when Mam decided to bring our old gramophone into Barry's auction in Academy Street and put whatever small amount of money it fetched towards a better one. The new one, a handsome His Master's Voice was contained in an oak cabinet and had a tiny white brush on the needle-arm that cleaned the dust off the record ahead of the needle. The gramophone had to be kept hidden under the bed, however, because Gran, who sorely missed our company and was always coming up to see us, would not approve of spending money in what she considered to be such an extravagant manner. So whenever the gramophone was being played one of us was posted at the end of the lane with strict orders that if Gran appeared on her way up Ninety Eight Street the alarm was to be raised. Whenever it was raised the gramophone was hastily returned to its hiding place behind the valance which covered the bed right down to the floor. We knew that if Gran ever became aware of its existence her immediate question to Mam would be: 'How much did that thing cost?' and if Mam were to tell her Gran would retort: 'You must be off your head to pay that much for it. Wouldn't the one you have do you and you could have put the money to better use.'

We quickly got to know everybody in Gunpowder Lane and became aware of the wonderful community spirit that existed amongst the families that lived there, about eight of them on our side and twenty on the other. They required nobody to inculcate that spirit in them. It was part and parcel of their make-up and had been handed down to them from generation to generation. If that spirit has been eroded somewhat in recent years it is mainly because people's houses are now built further apart and there is less dependence on one another. It is the way of life that has changed, not the people. The families in the lane knew no fear because the lane was narrow and little went unnoticed. Even at night one could hear the footsteps of people passing by and recognise most of them. Late one night there was a knock on our door. Mam answered. The caller was a man whom she had never seen before. He stood looking at her for a moment and then said: 'You're not the woman at all.'

'What woman?' said Mam.

'I was in a pub earlier tonight drinking with a woman and she told me if I came up I'd get a night's lodgings, but I must have the wrong house.'

Before he could say any more and before Mam had time to shut the door two doors across the lane opened almost simultaneously. A man appeared at one and a woman at the other.

'What are you looking for?' said the man across the way.

The stranger started to spin his yarn but hadn't got very far when he was sharply informed that there was no such woman in the lane and most certainly not in our house. He moved off but mustn't have succeeded in getting the comfortable lodgings which he had been led to expect because early next morning Mam spotted him leaving the outdoor toilet at the back of our house, obviously having endured an all-night's sitting there!

The area all around us was a maze of lanes many of which have long since disappeared. I can clearly recall Coburn's Lane, Fuller's Lane, Brandy Lane known today as St Finbarr's Road, Malachy's Lane, Hospital Lane later called Ninety Eight Street, Warren's Lane, Pigott's Lane, Tom Murphy's Lane and Protestant Lane down by St Fin Barres Protestant Cathedral. Off Barrack Street ran O'Leary's Lane where many people were housed during the Great Famine, Rochford's Lane and Crowley's

Lane. The mention of those lanes never fails to awaken an intense feeling of nostalgia in the many fine people who spent their young days in them and who hopefully now enjoy better conditions. Our lane was tiled in a beautiful pinky-red colour with a channel running down the middle, and when on a sunny summer's day a shower might fall the water heated by the tiles ran down that channel and all the children went paddling barefoot in it.

Both the men and the women in the lane could turn their hand to anything to make a few shillings. They might well be described as entrepreneurs but of course that is a term that was not destined to be part of the vocabulary of Irish people for many years to come. At the top of the lane there lived a man named Ring who was an ardent follower of St Finbarr's hurling team. He eked out a living mending shoes and making hurling balls, or sliotars as they are generally known. A good sliotar cost a shilling. Two other men were engaged in cutting timber to sell as firewood. When the Corporation trimmed the large trees in the Mardyke and other areas of the city those men bought the trimmings, carted them home to an alleyway where with the aid of a trestle and a cross-cut they sawed them into tidy blocks to be sold by the shilling's worth. Across the lane from us was the Scotsman who grew tomatoes in window-boxes. I was then blissfully ignorant of tomatoes and one day when the Scotsman's attention was diverted I decided to pick a green one and try it for taste. I desperately wanted to spit it out again, but afraid of what the consequences might be if he saw me, I grinned and swallowed it. Little wonder that to this day I have a strong aversion to tomatoes.

Another man who was gifted with his hands made small timber houses that were in great demand particularly by people who wished to use them as little bungalows near the sea at Youghal or Crosshaven. At that time no planning permission was required for such structures. They were beautifully finished with a door and windows. That man did his work in a cowluck and though he never locked his materials or tools away nobody ever stole a thing from him. He was a fine type of man and highly regarded. Just off the lane there was the fruit woman. During the war no foreign fruit was available so she experienced a marked increase in her business. She travelled to Bishopstown, Hangdog Road, Douglas and other areas buying apples from orchard owners. The apples were delivered to her house by donkey and cart. Mam's favourite apples were the 'mollies', small greenish yellow ones that to us tasted like honey. For sixpence she could buy enough to keep us going for days, but the birdpicks were even better value still. Rightly or wrongly we firmly believed that the birds chose only the sweetest ones to pick and so we rated the picks highly. If we had a penny or even a half-penny in our possession coming home from school we bought a few apples, and perhaps some child who didn't have any money would plead with another to give him the 'ox', by which he meant the heart of the apple.

The houses in Brandy Lane strangely enough had rather large gardens and many families grew a lot of rhubarb which they sold in armfuls for two pence each, including the fine fat shiny slugs which traced silvery lines all over the leaves. Very few children of our age today would relish rhubarb in a tart or as a Sunday dessert but we weren't spoiled for choice and found nothing wrong with it provided there was plenty of sugar to go with it. People in those days regarded it as a wonderful purgative, believing it cleaned one's inside just as effectively as it cleaned aluminium saucepans.

A strong sense of religion pervaded the lives of our community. People believed in God and valued their faith; yet they weren't slow in talking up to a priest if they considered him a bit too narky. Every family was attentive to their prayers and the Rosary was often recited in our house at night. We didn't have rosary beads however. We simply didn't have the money to buy them as almost every penny we possessed went on food and clothing. So it was with most families. The Eucharistic Procession which took place on the Sunday after the feast of Corpus Christi was the most public display of religious fervour of the whole year, when the men of the city marched in their thousands from their respective parishes to the Grand Parade for an open-air sermon and Benediction. As the men wended their way through the various roads and streets festooned with bunting the women watched them from the footpaths because they were not allowed to join in the procession. The days and weeks beforehand saw a transformation in the lanes. The men were busy with their buckets of yellow ochre and brushes decorating the outside walls of the houses as one would with whitewash. Then buckets of tar were produced, and indeed shared, to tar the bottom of the walls. Some households might paint their houses in a colour other than yellow ochre, and that served to heighten the effect, but we resented the actions of a few odd people who used dark gloomy colours. The few days before the procession was a busy time for Mam as neighbours asked her to make coloured flags. These flags were made of crepe paper which she cut into diamonds, yellow and white representing the papal colours, and red, a colour we all loved. We just had to have red. Anyhow wasn't it the Cork colour? Then with her sewing machine she ran the diamonds on to a white tape one inch wide, and the completed flags were strung across the lane from house to house on the eve of the procession. Everyone prayed that no rain would fall during the night because if it did the dye in the red crepe would run and a stream as if of blood would fill the channel. The inhabitants of the lane vied with one another to see who would have the best arranged altar in their window. Statues and holy pictures were placed on white cloths and surrounded by flowers many of which were taken from gardens in the richer suburbs without the owners' consent. In mitigation of the crime, however, it could be said that the cause was a noble one!

At that time ecumenism hadn't even been heard of, and though we passed up and down by St Fin Barres Protestant Cathedral – St Barries to us – we never went into it, and even had we wished to do so we would not be allowed. That situation thankfully has changed. Still we took a great pride in the cathedral being in our area, and always admired its beautiful architecture, from the outside of course!

One day about a year after we had gone to live in the lane Dad complained of a violent inner pain. He sent my mother down to the Dispensary in Liberty Street for a tonic but when she described his symptoms to the doctor he said: 'From what you tell me I cannot prescribe for your husband. I'll have to see him.'

'Doctor,' she said, 'I did everything in my power to get him to visit you but he refused.'

'Very well then,' said the doctor, who was an extremely caring person, 'I'll call to see him at home. Will he be there at tea-time?'

My mother assured him that he would. She knew better than to inform Dad of the arrangement, and just as he was about to sit down to his tea the doctor arrived. Having brought Dad down to the bedroom to examine him, he ordered that he be immediately removed to St Finbarr's Hospital, which Southsiders knew as 'The Union' while the Northsiders for some unknown reason called it 'Ger Gurr's'. Within the next day or two he was operated on, for the removal of a growth we were told. We visited him regularly but nobody held out much hope for his recovery, with the result that Mam was advised to buy a habit for him. She bought it from the nuns in St Marie's of the Isle Convent for thirty shillings, a pound and fifty pence in today's money. One day after Mam had come back from the hospital she told us that she had detected an improvement in Dad's condition and that she understood from him that he had had an egg for his tea.

'What will I do with the habit,' she said to my aunt, 'if please God he recovers?'

To lift her spirits my aunt answered: 'Can't you make pants for the boys out of it? It is a fine brown serge material and will wear well.'

The boys never got their brown serge pants, however, because on a Saturday afternoon three weeks after he had entered hospital Dad passed away at the age of thirty-seven, leaving a wife and seven children ranging from eleven years right down to the baby who had not yet reached his first birthday. The moment Gran heard of Dad's death she called to our house and insisted that we immediately go to stay with her, mainly to help Mam recover from the trauma caused by the bereavement. On the following Monday, to the sad tolling of the Lough Chapel bell, his remains were brought down Brandy Lane, through Gilabbey Street, down the quays of the South Jetty and out to St Joseph's Cemetery more commonly known as the 'Paranas'. The family travelled behind the hearse in a splendid carriage drawn by two beautifully-tackled black horses. When the carriage halted outside Gran's house in Gilabbey Street I peeped out between the blinds on the window and saw the horses stamping the concrete road impatiently and knocking sparks out of it as they waited to be off on their sad journey. We were all riven with sorrow, yet because of the darkness in the carriage I got an urge to pull back the curtain and peep out to view the passing scene, but a quick rap on the knuckles from Gran soon dampened my curiosity. Shortly after the funeral Mam considered it wise for us to return to the old house in Gunpowder Lane rather than remain on in Gran's because the new Corporation houses in Greenmount were nearing completion and we had applied for one. Thoughtful as ever Gran gave up the comfort of her own feather bed and came up each night to sleep with us. A stretcher bed was set up for her in the kitchen every night. It was just a spring mesh stretched across a timber frame. At each end two pieces of timber were screwed together in the form of a cross to act as legs but on occasions those legs were wont to collapse and Gran would suddenly be brought down to earth. Nevertheless she remained with us until such time as we became used to not having Dad around.

Shortly after his death his clothes were returned to us from St Finbarr's Hospital. In the pocket of his coat Mam found two shillings and eight pence, the sum total of his worldly riches after thirty-seven years on this earth. Not being able to bring

18

herself to spend the money she placed it in an unused tea-pot in the glass case and as the years went by the silver coins blackened while the copper ones turned green. During the subsequent couple of weeks the guards called twice to the house to arrest him for not attending his LDF gun-practice meetings in Catfort, the official name of which was Barrack Street Garda Barracks.

On receiving the dead money from the insurance company Mam wasted no time in paying off the funeral bills. One evening she put the money for the priest, Fr O'Toole, in an envelope and brought it up to the Lough Presbytery. As the priest was not at home she gave the money to his housekeeper. She had scarcely arrived back home again when the door was pushed in and Fr O'Toole appeared in the kitchen. Placing the envelope on the table he said to Mam: 'You need the money far more than I do. There's a long hard road in front of you but with God's help you and your family will travel it.'

He then turned and walked out. His gesture was of course much appreciated but then it was typical of the man. The return of the money, small though it was, helped to ease Mam's problems for a while. When she applied for the widow's pension soon afterwards she ran into unexpected difficulties because only then did she realise that Dad's employer had not been stamping his cards, which left us entitled only to the non-contributory pension of twenty-six shillings a week, whereas the contributory pension was worth thirty-three shillings, a very sizeable difference. Mam refused to accept the non-contributory pension. Pressure was brought to bear on the employer, and while negotiations were going on the Home Assistance Officer arranged for Mam to be given a weekly docket which permitted her to get food to the value of seventeen shillings in a specified shop. Grim days were ahead and I recall that on many an occasion she managed to provide us children with a boiled egg each while she made do with bread and tea, but we insisted that she at least take the tops of the eggs from us.

She decided to approach a TD in the city in an endeavour

to speed up the pension. Knowing where he resided she went there and knocked on the door. His wife answered and enquired about the nature of her business with him. Then she informed Mam that her husband was not at home. As Mam was about to leave a fine figure of a man, as she described him later, arrived at the door and asked the TD's wife if her husband was at home. Turning into the hallway the woman called her husband by his Christian name. Then Mam realised that even in the eyes of the public representatives some people counted more than others. Struggling to stem the tears she headed for home and her bread and tea. A day or two later a friend suggested that she put her case in the hands of a man living on the Northside. She did so and was treated with the utmost compassion and courtesy, and to her great relief she was able to begin drawing her contributory pension within a matter of days. Her faith in the generosity and kindness of people had been restored.

Razza and Wren Boys

Though money was scarce children led a comfortable and sheltered life and parents were very protective. Rarely were small children allowed to cry because there was always a grandmother or aunt in the house to assist the mother in minding them. Willing arms were stretched out to comfort a cross child while the mother was looking after the rest of the brood.

'Give her here to me and I'll give you a break,' the grandmother or aunt would say, and taking the child she would wrap her shawl around her and pace the floor up and down, all the while crooning or singing a lullaby.

Leaving the sanctuary of the home at four or five years of age and going out to school was a major shock to most children, so much so that some mothers would not enrol their offspring in school until the age of six. 'The child isn't rough enough yet to attend' was the reason usually given. Boys had a particular aversion to school and its discipline and it was not at all uncommon to see them being dragged through the streets and screaming their heads off. It was all to no avail, however, because parents were in mortal terror of their children being taken from them and put into an institution if they failed to send them to school. We heard about one boy who would not succumb to such public ignominy and whose parents couldn't trust him to attend on his own, so each morning they would tie him into a large potato sack with just his head protruding, then heave him up on a horse and cart and drive him to school.

Mam believed in packing her children off at four years of age. The nearest school to us was St Marie's of the Isle in Bishop Street just a few hundred yards away and run by the Sisters of Mercy who also had another school, St Aloysius', around the corner in Sharman Crawford Street for the children of better-off families. Gran always referred to St Aloysius' as the Pension School because it was said that the children of British soldiers had their education there paid for by the British government. St Marie's of the Isle catered for almost one thousand girls and boys. However the boys were allowed to remain there only until they received their First Holy Communion. There were over forty pupils in each class.

On my first day in St Marie's of the Isle my heart leapt for joy because all around the classroom just out of reach of our small hands were dolls, storybooks, shells and buckets of sand, but soon I was to realise that they were there only to be admired. I settled into school life reasonably quickly and soon became accustomed to the daily routine. The school had spacious playgrounds and in one of them was a corrugated iron shed called the 'Cocoa House'. When the *sos* or break came the poorer children queued up at the door for their enamel mugful of hot cocoa – those mugs we called ponnies – and a round of dry currant bread. Not all of the children availed of the food but for many of them it was their first meal of the day. Years later my mother recalled for me what another mother had said to her: 'Madge,' she said, 'many's the morning my children had to face school without a bite of bread or a mouthful of tea in their stomachs. I couldn't stop thinking about them as they went out to school, and after a while I'd sit down and will the hands of the clock around to eleven o'clock. Then I'd feel the life coming back into me again because I knew they'd be getting their bread and cocoa at that time.'

At Christmas each year the nuns arranged a poor children's party. The partitions between the classrooms were pushed back and the children seated at tables all around the enlarged area. The nuns were marvellous cooks and baked the daintiest cakes and scones which we devoured and washed down with home-made lemonade provided in white enamel buckets. The nuns then went around the tables and gave each child a fistful of sweets from silver-coloured tins held under their arms, butter nuggets, bull's-eyes, clove rocks and other mixtures. They also distributed toys and storybooks that had been donated by past pupils who had got on in the world. I clearly recall my first Christmas party. A large doll, the most beauti‣ful I had ever seen, had been presented to the school as a prize to be won by some lucky child. As it sat there on the windowsill each child's heart longed to win it for there was no chance that their parents could afford such a beautiful specimen. A nun announced that she would write on the back of the swivel-board a number between one and fifty, and that the child who guessed the correct number would win the doll. The nun who was my teacher was standing beside me. She bent down and whispered in my ear 'Say twenty-nine', so when my turn came I did as she bade me and piped up 'twenty-nine'. When the blackboard was swivelled around for us all to see there before us was a curvy two and a fine rounded nine. I had won the doll! My moment of glory had come. I was surrounded by envious classmates oohing and aahing at my treasured possession, and sticky little hands lifted up the pink star-studded dress to gaze in wonder at the delicate lace underwear, but all I wanted to do was to race home and examine the doll away from the hustle and bustle. As I grew older I was no longer allowed to attend the free Christmas party but somehow or other I always managed to secure a prize by getting one of the top six places in the Christmas examinations. I never did well enough to get first place, the prize for which was usually a new book. Secondhand books were awarded for the second and subsequent places, while each girl in the class received the gift of a holy picture stitched on to white cardboard and adorned with coloured sequins by the nuns.

All through my school years Granda was a great help and source of encouragement to me. He was also a man of infinite patience. As he sat in his shop stitching the uppers of shoes on to soles I used to learn my poetry. Then he would lay aside his work, take the poetry-book in his hand and listen to me while I recited the poem until I had it word-perfect. It was Granda's love for his country and the stories of his young days in Clonakilty that awakened my interest in the Irish language which I loved and later succeeded in mastering quite well. For most nuns and teachers I had a great admiration. They had our interests at heart, but their best endeavours on our behalf were often thwarted by children having to face into school without a pencil or a pen or a copybook and get the loan of a nib or a page from better-off classmates. There was unfortunately a small minority of nuns and teachers who were rather harsh and lacking in understanding. Girls taught by them usually tried to console themselves by saying: 'Don't mind that one. She must have been jilted in her day.' In fifth class I had the misfortune to be taught by a nun who for some reason unknown to me had a habit of making me stand up in class and then ridiculing me in front of the other girls. That cut me to the quick and was worse than a dozen slaps. Indeed she never slapped us but used her tongue to chastise us. I must give her due credit, however, for inculcating in me a love of reading. For half an hour every Friday she read for us excerpts from Canon Sheehan's *Glenanaar*, and during those periods I felt the hurt disappear as I soaked into my soul the love of literature. My most bitter and embarrassing experience in school was having to get a free copy of *Stair na hEorpa* from the nuns because Mam could not afford to buy it. On the inside cover was pasted a form stating: 'This book is the property of St Marie's of the Isle Convent. If it is defaced or torn the borrower must replace it with a new copy.' When other children enquired why such a form was attached to my book I blushed with shame and burying my hands in my face I refused to answer.

Christmas was undoubtedly the highlight of the year for both young and old, even though it was an expensive time for already hard-pressed parents. However they never complained of bad times or scarcity of work as long as they had Christmas to look forward to. They were quite prepared to skimp and scrape so as to have a few pounds to spend for the festive season. Those at work would join a diddle-um at their place of employment. The diddle-um commenced at the beginning of January and one of the workers was selected to take over the running of it. Members would hand over one penny each to that person on the first payday of January. The next payday the subscription would be two pence, and each week it increased by a penny until the final subscription of four shillings and four pence. The total subscribed over the year amounted to nearly six pounds, a considerable sum. Workers often found it hard to pay as the payments rose, yet they almost invariably persevered until the end. They drew their diddle-ums a week before Christmas and brought the money home, and that money made it possible for the mother to buy ham, roast pork and all the other things that went with Christmas. It would also enable her to buy tarpaulin for the kitchen and about six rolls of wallpaper to decorate the house. The tarpaulin being of the cheaper kind cost only about thirty shillings and within eight to ten weeks the design would have worn off it. The wallpaper was always bought from Stevie O'Mahony's in Barrack Street.

Another method employed by workers to ensure that they had money for Christmas or indeed for any other occasion was known as the 'manage'. It differed from the diddle-um in that a set amount of money was paid in each week, two shillings or five shillings or more depending on one's pay. It was different also in that it usually ran over a shorter period. Ten people might agree to subscribe ten shillings a week for ten weeks, a total of five pounds weekly from the very first week. Each subscriber was allotted a number between one and ten. The person who collected the money and took care of it was given the privilege of being Number One, and the remaining nine drew numbers from two to ten out of a hat. Number One received five pounds at the end of the first week, Number Two received the same amount at the end of the second week and so it went on until Number Ten received his or her five pounds at the end of the tenth week. It was an ingenious way of providing financial assistance when most needed, because a person who might urgently need such assistance could offer to become the collector and therefore be Number One. There was seldom if ever a defaulter while no collector was ever known to defraud.

In addition to the fare brought with the aid of the diddle-um or the manage, families could also look forward to a Christmas present from the local shopkeeper in appreciation of their custom. A good customer usually received a large square Killarney fruitcake wrapped in silver paper with a red band around it. That was accompanied by a pound Christmas candle which was known to all as a 'pounder'. A less valued customer received a smaller Killarney cake and a candle, but the person who called in only sporadically was given just the smaller cake. The difference between the presents always posed a headache for the shopkeeper who understandably did not wish to hurt the feelings of any customer. If there were a few people in the shop at any given time – and those shops were quite small – it was no easy matter for the shopkeeper to slip the larger cake and candle undetected to one customer in the presence of another not so highly esteemed, and despite his best ruses he was not always successful in avoiding the disaffection and indeed the loss of some customers. Luckily for us my mother always qualified for the large cake and candle and knowing how we loved any sort of cake she would also buy a seed cake to tide us over the holidays.

As Christmas approached the children would go around the streets chanting outside the door of each house:

> Christmas is coming, the goose is getting fat.
> Please put a penny in the poor man's hat.
> If you haven't got a penny a ha'penny will do.
> If you haven't got a ha'penny a piece of bread will do.
> If you haven't got a piece of bread may God bless you.

Every night for some time before Christmas the Salvation Army Band would visit streets and entertain the people with Christmas carol music. The Salvation Army in those years had a refuge in Pope's Quay where homeless men could seek shelter for the night for just a few pence.

On Christmas Eve Mam would gather all us children and complete with pram we would set off for town. Our first stop was the Coal Quay where she bought the red-berried holly and some ivy. These were considered to bring luck and so no house wished to be without them. Then she would go into the second-hand record shop nearby to purchase some records to play on Christmas Day. Impatiently we would stand by the pram outside while she rummaged through stacks of records in search of some of her favourites. Her next stop was Paul Street where she would order me to go into Kiloh's mineral waters shop for raspberry cordial, more familiarly known as razza.

'Here's a half-crown to give the man and tell him we have a shop.'

I would go in as I was told, go over to the counter and place the half-crown on it.

'A quart bottle of razza, please sir, and we have a shop.'

The man would hand me the square quart bottle at the wholesale price and for that half-crown our drinking needs for the Christmas season were secured. Mam never allowed intoxicating drink into the house. Every household in the area had razza for Christmas and even to this very day I have maintained the custom myself. Having got the razza she would then buy a good-sized piece of pork from Mackey's in the North Main Street and some bacon from O'Callaghan's just across the street. Using a long pole with a crook on the end of it the assistant would lift the piece of bacon off a hook on the ceiling. She bought it only if it was Cork-cured because she considered the up-country bacon far too salty. The pram would be filling up by this time but we still had to call to Glass's shop in Patrick Street to buy oilcloth for the kitchen table. The pattern on the oilcloth was always the same, black grapes, green grapes, rosy red apples, green apples, golden oranges and clusters of yellow bananas.

Our last trip was to Woolworths where Mam purchased a few small items from the sixpenny counter downstairs. Three wide stone staircases, made of concrete which appeared to glitter, led up to the first floor where what seemed to our minds like an Aladdin's cave of toys was the great attraction. I loved to gaze at the doll-counter which displayed double-jointed dolls of every shape and size, chaney dolls dressed in silken fabrics and gelatine dolls with real feathers dyed in brilliant shades of cerise, emerald, blue and pink, covering certain parts of their anatomy in the interests of decency. Hornby train sets, motor cars and fire engines filled another counter. However, children of my generation realised only too well that the limitations on our parents' purses made it impossible to purchase such toys except perhaps at Christmas and so we were satisfied with just being able to view them.

We would plead with our mothers: 'Hoist me up, Mam, I want to see the toys.' We were always brought to see Daddy Christmas, and were thrilled when he emerged from his red-bricked paper house to wave at us. We were surprised that he was so small in stature, however, until we realised that Woolworth's Daddy Christmas was indeed a woman! Thank heavens we never envied the children of well-off parents who could visit him in his house and later reappear with coloured parcels under their arms. We had to be patient until Christmas morning when he came down our chimney with whatever few toys he had for us. It was only then our dreams were fulfilled. Little did I realise, though, the trouble to which Mam went in her annual pre-Christmas search for damaged toys which she would then repair in time for delivery by Santa himself. Those toys might include a gelatine doll with only one hand. Mam would re-attach the other hand to the body with white elastic thread. If the doll had a bruise on its body she would stick a darning needle into the dent and smooth it out leaving only a tiny hole showing. If she came across a motor car with one wheel missing she searched the whole counter until she found the wheel. Finding a replacement for a missing dice in a box of games presented no problem as a substitute dice could be bought elsewhere for a few pence. A tin of children's paints complete with brush but missing one or two of the colours was usually available at half-price. We were quite pleased with our seconds and Mam's burden was eased because her money went so much further.

For some unfortunate families the hustle and bustle of

shopping on Christmas Eve wouldn't yet have begun. Many a mother would have to wait for her husband to come home with the wages, while some might have to search the pubs for the husbands and bring them home. Others still in very poor circumstances might have to borrow money. They would all have to do their shopping in nearby Barrack Street. That meant that the shops there were open until all hours.

Mam would have made the Christmas pudding a day or two before Christmas. There was never a bowl to make a pudding large enough to satisfy our appetites, so having mixed all the ingredients together she would shape it with her hands and flour the pillow-slip which was to act as a superbowl. This flouring left a fine skin on the outer side of the pudding when cooked, like a baby's bottom we always said. She would then put the pudding into the pillow-slip and tie the corners of the slip so that a bockety odd-shaped specimen would not result. She would then plunge the pillow-slip, cake and all into boiling water for a few hours and the resultant skin acted as a seal thus preventing any water from getting into the pudding. When it was cooked she took it up and hung it, still in the pillow-slip, from the ceiling. Very soon the skin would be quite hard and when Mam's back was turned the boys would start tapping it with a hurley or firing darts at it to test its resistance.

After nightfall on Christmas Eve we would light the pounder Christmas candle which might be either red or white. We preferred the red one as we felt it was more traditional but it had the disadvantage of being much more inclined to drip. We then put some tinsel around the candle which stood in a jampot and stuck a sprig of holly with red berries into it near the base. That was a sight to delight even the most sophisticated. It was then time to sit down to tea. There was, however, no question of having meat with the tea because Christmas Eve was a day of fast and abstinence and nobody disobeyed that rule.

We could do without the meat, however, but not without the sultana cake. Christmas to us was the sultana cake. We just gorged ourselves on it. We never had a home-made Christmas cake of our own because we had only the open fire for cooking and baking a cake was not possible. When we lived with my grandparents Gran would prepare a meal of crubeens and parsnips on Christmas Eve for the adults of the family on their arrival home from Midnight Mass about half-past one in the morning. After we moved to our house in the lane Gran still roasted our pork for us since we did not have an oven in which to roast it ourselves. I can still clearly see her as she used her knife to remove the covers off the toes of the crubeens. We loved to fit those covers on our fingers like thimbles. She would then put the crubeens and parsnips into a pot and boil them into babby-rags, as we used to say, that is into pulp. That is the right way to cook crubeens.

We children were then ushered back upstairs to bed but of course we didn't forget to hang up our stockings on the fireplace. Next morning we were up before dawn. Our living-room had been transformed since the previous night, because while we slept Mam put the red-berried holly and ivy behind all the pictures and gilded some of the picture-frames so that they glowed a golden colour. The strange but welcome smell of the new oilcloth on the freshly scrubbed timber was the first thing to attract our attention. Then there was the beautiful little coloured cardboard crib. We never had a Christmas tree, however. The mantelpiece was covered with a red plush cloth to which woollen baubles had been attached and the fireplace limed while its surround was newly painted cherry-red. But we children had eyes only for our stockings on the fireplace and what they contained. Daddy Christmas never brought us very much, a small toy perhaps, an orange, an apple, a few sweets, a small paper packet of sultanas if there were any left over after making the pudding. We might get a couple of pencils, a cheap colouring book or a game of ludo. In the toe of each stocking would be a brand new golden Irish penny with the hen and clutch of chickens on one side and the harp on the other. The presents amounted to very little but we never complained because those which the children all around us got were very similar to ours. Our joy knew no bounds, and we wouldn't call the queen our aunt.

Later on in the morning we would go to Mass and Holy Communion in the Lough Chapel but it was always extremely hard to concentrate. For dinner we would have bacon and a bit of pork along with plenty of floury potatoes. If money was flush there might also be a piece of silverside corned beef. Of course there was always the cabbage. No house would be without cabbage for dinner any Sunday or special feast-day such as Christmas Day. We all loved pork, particularly the cracknel which was biscuit-like pieces of fat fried crisp. We would eat a *taoscán* of pork about which the older people used to say ''Tis grand; 'tis like chicken,' and you wouldn't mind but they would not eat chicken if they got it for nothing! We delighted in potato stuffing but bread stuffing meant absolutely nothing to us. The meal was rounded off with a bowl of jelly.

We never had a turkey in those days, nor indeed did any of the neighbours, but when some of my brothers and sisters and myself went out to work perhaps we got notions as one year we gave Mam the money to buy a turkey for us. She cooked it, but all to no avail because we refused to eat it, particularly the black meat, and so it was given to the dogs who didn't seem to have any qualms about either the meat or its colour. As for the stuffing you put into a bird we wouldn't insult our palate with it.

A similar fate befell the goose which my father won playing cards one Christmas in Miss O's pub. All shopkeepers and publicans were known to their customers as Mr O, Mrs O and Miss O depending on their marital status. When Mam cooked the goose nobody would eat it so the dogs in the cowluck had the Christmas goose all for themselves. Fowl meat of any sort was anathema to the old Corkonians and only in later years have some of them taken to eating it at all.

After dinner was a time for rest and relaxation. My father would stretch himself across the double bed in the room to read the Cork *Holly Bough,* a Christmas magazine produced by the *Cork Examiner,* and it was required reading in every home for the festive season. Mam would put on the gramophone. It was not unlike an attaché case. Having placed the box of silver needles beside it she would then take the records down from the top of the glass case. Some of them were in light brown paper covers while others were in heavy cardboard covers. The twelve-inch records were mostly of music from the operas and the eight-inch ones were of the popular singers of the day. Each time Mam placed a record on the turntable she would have to wind up the spring of the gramophone and change the needle. Failure to change the needle was regarded as a serious omission and rightly so, because it caused the record to be scratched and permanently damaged. Sometimes in the middle of an aria on the twelve-inch record the gramophone would slow down with a wah-wah-wah sound. That was the signal for Mam to rush to its aid and turn the handle again to increase the speed. If the gramophone was over-wound the spring would break, and there was nothing for it then but put it into the baby's pram and bring it down to Bachelor's Quay, where a man had a room in his house set aside for the repairing of gramophones and children's prams. For renewing a spring he charged one shilling, that is five pence in today's money.

The records featuring the comedian Jimmy O'Dea were very popular with us children and indeed with most of the children in the area. They were dialogue rather than music records: 'Casey at the Dentist', 'Casey in the Pawnshop', 'Casey in the Betting Shop' and 'Casey at the Wake'. The ubiquitous Casey never ceased to delight us no matter how often we heard him. We also had an Anne Boleyn record which chilled us with its ghostly music, and from which I recall just the following lines:

> With her head tucked underneath her arm
> She walks the bloody tower,
> With her head tucked underneath her arm
> At the midnight hour.

'The Laughing Policeman' was another favourite as was John McCormack's rendering of 'Little Boy Blue' though it was likely to reduce some of us to tears. Jigs, reels and hornpipes would set our feet tapping on the floor, and of all of them the Sailor's Hornpipe was the one we liked best. All the while we sated ourselves with currant cake and razza which had to be diluted with water, and a shuttle service was required to go and refill the kettle from the tap in the backyard.

On Christmas night we would join our grandparents and aunts and uncles around the fire. Gran would provide more food and insist on everyone having a piece of her loin of pork out of their hand. Then she would tell us of various events that she associated with previous Christmasses. One of them concerned a Christmas morning when she and her family had just arrived home from Mass. They had scarcely taken their coats off when there was a knock on the door. It was their neighbour Mary Kate with some broken bits of porter-cake wrapped in the *Echo*.

'Take this,' says Mary, 'The kids might eat it.'

Placing the parcel on the table she blurted out her story.

'That husband of mine came home stotious last night. I took one look at his condition and I went baldheaded for him. I looked around for something to throw at him and the nearest thing to my hand was the porter-cake that was just after coming out of the oven. I flung it at him and hit him right on the kisser. And after all that, he had the gall to tell me he was one of the best husbands in Cork! Maybe the kids will eat the cake because I have no stomach for it now.'

Such were the joys of Christmas for some couples!

Before going to bed the last thing to be done was to put a few pennies – coppers we usually called them – on the mantelpiece in readiness for the wren boys next morning, St Stephen's Day.

About six o'clock that morning loud banging on the doors of the neighbourhood announced the arrival of the wren boys, young lads from about ten years of age upwards, and their raucous rendering of 'The wren, the wren, the king of all birds' would result in mothers leaping out of their beds, grabbing a penny from the mantelpiece and throwing it out the window to get rid of the wren boys before they awakened their husbands and children. They were also anxious not to incur the displeasure of the wren boys by refusing them money because if they did they would then be subjected to a derogatory verse reserved for such an occasion:

> Mrs O'Sullivan is a holy woman
> Who goes to Mass on Sunday.
> She prays to God for half-a-crown
> When she visits the pawn on Monday.

There was one cranky old man who lived in Friar's Walk and detested all wren boys. He always rose early on St Stephen's morning to heat some pennies on a shovel in the fire and then took a fiendish delight in throwing them out the window and watching the wren boys pick them up and get their fingers burnt. The wren boys generally ceased their caterwauling about ten o'clock and then it was time to share between them the money which they had collected. This share-out provided them with the wherewithal to get into the special midday matinees for children in the Palace and Coliseum cinemas, and usually left them with enough to give their sisters who would come scrounging the admission fee off them. On entering the cinemas each child received a small paperful of sweet mixtures and this little act of generosity ensured a full house.

All picture houses were packed on St Stephen's Day with long queues outside their doors and some patrons failing to gain admission. Cowboy pictures and those of the swash-buckling type were much more popular than slushy romantic ones. Comedies also drew large crowds. There were various pantomimes too in the Opera House, Fr Matthew Hall, the AOH Hall, St Francis' Hall, Fr O'Leary Hall and St Vincent's Hall, but the admission fee to even the cheapest of these was ninepence whereas that of the cinemas was as low as three-

34

pence. Consequently only people in employment could afford to patronise the pantomimes. As a child I never saw one and had to wait until such time as I was fully grown and had a job to be able to afford it.

In spite of all the gaiety and hilarity associated with St Stephen's Day no family forgot the holy season that was in it. They all visited the crib in the church, perhaps even in a few churches and a common topic of conversation was the merits of the respective cribs. Many conscientious husbands too marked the day by abstaining from drink as they did not wish to upset their wives and children by running the risk of arguments or fights. Others, of course, would overindulge and come home sozzled.

On St Stephen's Night there were dances in every hall in the city and all the younger people went dancing. How we envied them as we watched them go out dressed in all their finery but dancing was something which we children would have to wait some years to experience.

On New Year's Eve the Christmas candle was lit and a long-standing custom observed. A minute after midnight all the doors in the area were opened. The housewives emerged from their homes with a loaf of bread in their hands and with this they would beat on the doors calling out at the same time 'A Happy New Year'. This ritual they performed in the firm belief that it ensured their families would have sufficient food right through the coming year. Shandon's Bells would ring out over the city and the ships in the harbour added to the din by hooting their foghorns. People also believed that if a dark-haired man was the first to cross their threshold just after the birth of the New Year luck would follow him into the house and remain there for the year, so every household endeavoured to have such a man waiting outside the door ready for the moment when Shandon's Bells commenced their chimes.

The feast of the Epiphany was known in Cork, and indeed in many other places, as the Poor Women's Christmas. The Christmas candle was again lit on that night. There is an old saying in Irish *'Nollaig na bhFear Nollaig mhór mhaith agus Nollaig na mBan Nollaig gan mhaith'*, which translated means 'The men's Christmas [25 December] is a fine big Christmas and the Women's Christmas is no good'. This was usually understood to mean that after all the money spent on luxuries for Christmas Day there was very little left to purchase anything for the Women's Christmas. It could also have arisen from the fact that the dainties which women usually preferred, tea and cakes and such like, were cheaper and less appealing to men. The older women who were partial to a drop of drink went out to the pubs and gathered not in the main bar but in the snug which was a small section specially partitioned off for the exclusive privacy of women. A hatch in the partition enabled them to purchase their drink out of the sight of prying eyes. The men would often send them a 'whacker' or half of a half-glass of brandy in through the hatch in honour of the occasion.

The women in our house honoured the Epiphany by cleaning and scrubbing the kitchen until it gleamed like a new pin. Then a glass of water was placed on the table in readiness for Our Lord who would visit the house during the night, in remembrance of His first miracle when He turned water into wine at the wedding feast of Cana. Everybody had to be in bed before midnight, and if any of us displayed any reluctance to do so we were reminded of the story concerning the man who once boasted that he was staying up to see the Lord, and was found dead in his chair by the fire the following morning. He had died, we were told, at the moment of the miracle. We duly obliged and went to bed in good time. Next morning the glass of water was taken outside and emptied down the shore.

POTTER-UPS, DRISHEENS, DUGGY AND BATTLEBOARD

Some families in our neighbourhood were more affected by poverty than others and found it extremely difficult to make ends meet. Occasionally a distraught mother without any bread in the house and too ashamed to admit to her plight might send one of her children to a neighbour's door to ask for any heels of bread that might be left over. These were for her husband's breakfast next morning. Many is the husband and father of a young family who left his home at first light on an empty stomach, not to go to work but in search of work, usually down the docks, and as often as not returned home unsuccessful and still fasting. We ourselves were possibly slightly better off than most because of Mam's earnings as a dressmaker, meagre though they were. In spite of sometimes overwhelming poverty parents made every effort to ensure that their children got the best food they could afford.

Dinner was the meal which enabled the thrifty housewife to show her inventiveness in providing nourishing food cheaply. A dinner without potatoes was unimaginable because, apart from being cheap, potatoes also were filling and a great favourite of men, women and children. We always bought ours, sixpence worth at a time, from the proprietor of Kelleher's shop on the South Main Street. He was known to us as 'The Countryman' and we respected him because he always gave good weight. From him too we bought our 'potter-ups' – a couple of carrots, a leek, a few sticks of celery, a bit of thyme and a white turnip, a vegetable now rarely seen on any table. The term 'potter-ups' was possibly a corruption of the word pot-herbs.

All meat had to be boiled because in the absence of ovens cooking was done on the open fire. That in itself wasn't a great disadvantage inasmuch as boiled dinners were really nourishing and economical for a large family. A shilling's worth of beef pieces was sufficient to provide a good dinner. The pieces were put into a pot of water, together with a pinch or two of salt and a good-sized marrowbone which one could get free from the butcher. The meat was then boiled and delicate members of the family were given a cupful of the broth and some bread. That was the beeftea of our day. Then it was time to put the potter-ups into the pot. When both meat and potter-ups were ready a cupful of the meat-water was taken from the pot and some pea-flour, ground peas that came in a red box from the shop, was mixed with it and then poured back into the pot to thicken the contents. Oxo or Erinox cubes were often used to colour it. None of the precious liquid was wasted and if it wasn't taken as soup then family members could dip their bread in it or pour it on their potatoes to moisten them. Sometimes pearl barley, reputedly good for the kidneys, or a fistful of flake meal was used to thicken the liquid. I recall people often telling us how the poorest of their generation used to eat boiled cows' paps. These were known as 'duggy', and it is said that they tasted fine and could be sliced just like cheese. Nowadays, of course, nobody eats duggy because people have become too grand, and prefer pizzas, curries and the like. At least it could be said of duggy that when eating it you knew what you were eating.

Lamb or mutton rarely featured on our menu except that for the Sunday dinner Mam would buy four shillings' worth of lean lap of mutton which the butcher kept in the pickle-barrel until the Saturday. Some neighbours ate trotters, as sheep's feet were called. The trotters, however, were difficult and tedious to cook, but were considered by many to be a delicacy. Pig-meat was always a great favourite. I am not of course referring to the dearer cuts which were beyond our financial means, but rather loin-bones, skirts, bodices, handles and of course the inevitable pig's head and crubeens. A back-bone cost just three-pence and was always boiled with a turnip. It was chopped into smallish pieces and the white maggot-like spinal column had to be drawn from it with the aid of a strong fork before it was placed in the pot. The pig's tail was another delicacy, especially the fan which was nearest the animal's backside and was very meaty. Tripe, which is made from the lining of the sheep's stomach, and drisheen, which consists mainly of blood and tansy, figured high up in the list of preferences, although their popularity has in recent years declined somewhat, due perhaps to the relative affluence which people now enjoy.

Times have changed since my young days and so have people's tastes, something which was brought home forcefully to me only very recently. Two old Cork cronies paid a visit to a well-known supermarket and at the corner of one of the aisles a lady attired in a white coat was offering small samples of meat to customers. As the two old women were passing by she asked them if they would like to taste a sample.

'What sort of meat is that?' enquired one of them.

'That's venison,' replied the white-coated lady.

'God, what's that?' said the old woman. 'I'm buying meat for Christy all me life and I never heard of the like of that.'

Her companion interjected: 'Don't you know those reindeer, Maggie? They're Santa's horses. That's what it is.'

'I wouldn't dream of putting a thing like that in me mouth,' said the other woman, sauntering away.

The white-coated lady thought that maybe the term venison was not the one best calculated to gain the customer's interest, so when another old woman came along a few minutes later she asked her if she would like to taste a sample.

'What's that, love?' said the old woman.

'That's deer meat,' she was informed.

'I don't give a damn whether 'tis dear or cheap, just tell me what it is,' she replied, quite narked at the inference, as she saw it, that it was beyond her means.

Most families were very partial to fish though their lack of purchasing power led inevitably to their being limited to the cheaper kinds. The herring was arguably the most popular of all. 'Dip in the dip and let the herring for your Da' was a common saying. The herring was boiled with a liberal helping of onions and eaten with junks of bread dipped into the gravy in which it had been boiled. There was an art in purchasing the most desirable type of herring, an art of which even the most discerning of modern-day housewives might not be aware. When sent out to buy a herring one was always told to ask for 'the ones with the pea in them'. That was the female of the species. By running the thumb and first finger gently along the belly of the fish it was possible to detect which ones contained the pea, or the roe as it is generally known. These gravelly little eggs were always reserved for the man of the house because he had to be looked after, come hell or high water. Battleboard or salted ling was also in great demand. It was usually on display suspended from nails outside shop-doors, was hard as a board and required steeping overnight. Even then it was extremely salty but it was very popular among the men mainly because it gave them a thirst and so they relished their porter all the more afterwards.

Granda always maintained that sprats were the cleanest little fish in the sea because he had always heard that they never ate the bodies of the drowned. When in season they could be bought either from old women who sold them locally from a box-car or better still from the fishermen below on French's Quay where they were likely to be fresher. To cook them one cut their heads off with a scissors, cleaned out the tiny gut and boiled them with plenty of onions. When they were ready to eat the men picked them up in their hands, threw their heads back and devoured them bones and all. A feeling of nostalgia comes over me nowadays when I saunter down the quays and no longer see the fishermen with their navy blue jerseys and cloth caps tending their braziers, mending their nets and boiling the tar to caulk their little boats. These too were the men who, when the occasion arose, helped unstintingly in recovering the bodies of unfortunate people who had either fallen or thrown themselves into the river Lee.

Eating fowl was something unheard of in our community. People felt that there was no cutting in them and they wanted cutting. Little wonder is it then that I have never eaten a goose nor drunk chicken broth. Rarely have I eaten turkey, but nowadays I might reluctantly eat a bit of chicken now and then. Still I can pass by the chicken-laden counters in the Grand Parade Market without feeling the slightest inclination to buy one. Admittedly there were occasions when I scanned them closely, not because I harboured any thoughts of purchasing but strangely enough because of a friend of mine who, whenever she wanted to convey how little she worried about other people's opinions of her, was wont to say: 'I don't give a hen's titty about them!' I found the remark quite intriguing and wondered what the basis for it was, so for a while after first hearing it I would eye the chickens in the stalls as they looked up at me from the cold slabs and try to find out what was so unique about their mammary attributes, but far from noticing any such paraphernalia I couldn't see even a pimple on them! It was only on realising that chickens do not have titties that I understood fully the meaning of my friend's saying.

Granda always maintained that any young man thinking of matters matrimonial should take particular note of the way a girl made a cup of tea. 'Marry the girl who makes a fine strong cup,' he used to say, 'but stay clear of the one who makes it weak.' Tea rationing however, ordained that in our young days a girl didn't have a chance of proving herself one way or the other. In fact tea was so scarce that we often had to use cocoa instead. We bought our cocoa up in Phair's shop at the street junction still known as Phair's Corner. Each packet of Fry's cocoa contained a coupon and depending on the number of coupons collected and returned to Fry's one could in due course get various gifts through the post. For our tea we rarely had anything that might be even remotely termed a luxury except, perhaps, if money was a wee bit flush. Then Mam might send one of us up to Lyons' shop for six ounces of tinned beef. That was considered a treat.

The small hucksters shops around our area played a big part in the people's lives in those pre-supermarket days. Their owners knew each customer personally. They also knew each customer's financial situation and whether they were good payers or not. They were quite happy to sell goods on tick to people who required that facility. Those availing of tick were supplied with a notebook which they brought with them to the shop each time they wished to make a purchase. The shopkeeper then recorded the purchase in the notebook and kept a copy in his own ledger. Each weekend the customer cleared the account thus ensuring that she could buy her requirements the following week, but if a family encountered financial difficulties, particularly as a result of the father's unemployment, the shopkeeper allowed them tick until such time as the father got back to work. Then the accumulated arrears were whittled away week by week until the slate was clean once again. The majority of customers were very honourable and would not renege on their commitments.

It was quite common for housewives to have an account in two shops simultaneously because one shop might not stock the exact type or brand of groceries which they required. Mam operated tick in two shops in Gilabbey Street because she was partial to country butter and considered it superior to the creamery butter stocked by the shop where she usually dealt. The other shop, Hynes' at the corner of the street, sold country butter which was fresh and salted in rather large blocks. It was unwrapped. I loved to stand at the counter and watch the shopkeeper reach for the two timber clappers from an earthenware crock full of water, slice from the block the amount of butter required and dexterously pat it into an oblong shape with the aid of the clappers. Many women refused to allow shopkeepers to pat their butter in this manner and insisted in getting it in a lump no matter how ungainly it might appear. For some unknown reason they believed that it lost some of its flavour because of the patting or maybe because of the water on the clappers.

Nowadays powerful arguments are put forward about the respective merits of butter and margarine but I am convinced that most of the mothers during my childhood, were they to come back today, wouldn't touch margarine. Not even in our poorest days did Mam sit us down to the table with margarine on our bread. High quality dripping with plenty of beef sediment at the bottom of it was readily available in shops which purchased it from hotels and from the gentry in the big houses around the city and surrounding area. I have eaten bread fried in such dripping and found it quite palatable.

People rarely bought their milk in shops. It was delivered by horse and cart to the door mostly by men who farmed close to the city. In the cart there would be three or four large churns, each with a brass tap. There was a hole in the tail-board of the cart through which the tap protruded, thus enabling the milkman to fill a smaller hand-held churn until the milk bubbled in froth up to the brim. That churn he carried to the door and with a pint measure he poured the required amount into the jug or sweet-gallon or whatever other container the housewife proffered. The main advantage of buying from the milkman was that he always added a tilly or extra drop. He might also add a second tilly if there was a cat in the house or indeed he might pour it out on the floor for immediate consumption by the grateful feline. There were no carpets or other fancy coverings to worry about. Nobody had such a welcome for the milkman as the cat had, and that was evident from the way it purred appreciatively and rubbed itself against his trouser legs. All the while the horse waited patiently outside until it was ordered to move on to the next stop which it did without the milkman having to lay a hand on the reins – the original automatic pilot! One poor milk vendor I remember had only a jennet and I saw it after many years of faithful service drop down dead between the shafts of the cart. I also saw the tears run copiously down the vendor's cheeks as he undid the traces to lift the cart off the dead animal. He was so upset at the death of his faithful friend that subsequently he lost heart and disappeared altogether from our streets. Years later I was told that that same whiskery old man was one of the last Irish language poets of the Cork region.

The standard of milk was as varied as the number of farmers who supplied it, depending presumably on how well their cows were fed and cared for but that is not how all city people perceived it. After I married and went to live in the North Side I was one day walking out the Blarney Road with my children and a friend and noticed a stream by the roadside. 'That's the Mile Stream,' said the woman accompanying us, 'where the farmers used to stop to water the milk before selling it in the city.' I doubt if there was any basis for such a harsh judgement. More than likely it was because castigating farmers had become a sort of pastime with people in the city. Even if some farmers were inclined to practise such dishonesty it cannot have been easy for them to escape detection because quite often one could see government inspectors take samples from the various churns in the carts of milk vendors and bottling them for later laboratory analysis.

Children then as always were very sweet-mouthed and because the pocket money was so scarce we quickly learned how and where to get the best value for it. There was a small shop in Bandon Road where we used to buy six Cadbury chocolates for a penny. It didn't worry us that those chocolates were slightly mouldy and to my knowledge they never did us any harm. Across the road there was an old woman who made her own sweets known as Maggie Mannion's Candy. Maggie made her candy in full view of the customers and we often watched her pulling and stretching it while it was still hot and dividing it into small pieces. She then wrapped it up for us in a piece of newspaper. Neither her method of manufacture nor her premises would satisfy today's hygiene inspectors, I'm afraid. Across from Green Street was Dwyer's grocery shop which in addition to all the regular items also carried a stock of 'brus', small pieces of broken sweet mixtures and the scrapings from the bottom of the sweet-tins. The shop-owner would take a piece of newspaper, twirl it round her finger into the shape of a coronet, twist the narrow end to close it up, and then having put the 'brus' into the coronet she closed the broad end by simply folding over the top of the paper. Biscuits were sold loosely out of large tins and that resulted in some of them being broken in the handling. Those broken ones were sold for little or nothing but Mam advised us strongly against buying them. 'Look at them,' she would say. 'They're not clean breaks and they weren't broken in the shop but in the factory and then maybe they were walked on.' A doubting Thomas if ever there was one.

Simcox's shop in Paul Street and Darcy's in Oliver Plunkett Street were the places to buy cold cakes. For sixpence they sold a paperful of day-old or broken cakes. Gudge cake was a great favourite of ours. Gudge was a bread-pudding mixture with a thin layer of pastry on top and bottom. Mam was not too keen on it. She didn't like its dark colour and doubted the origins of its ingredients but we just loved its spicy flavour. There was plain gudge and there was gudge which had a white icing on top and was known as 'donkey's wedding cake'. The name might have put off lesser mortals but not us. Yet I must admit I had to draw the line one day at the sight of a shopkeeper cutting long bars of unmarked black and putty-coloured soap into sections with a knife and immediately afterwards using that same knife on the gudge cake. Albert cake was another favourite. It cannot have been too bad because Mam did not object to our indulging in it. It was yellow in colour and covered in white icing. A few doors up the street from our own house lived a woman who sold bread pudding by the halfpenny worth.

Sometimes, finances permitting, a few of us would pay a visit to Woolworths' Threepenny and Sixpenny Stores in the street known officially as St Patrick Street but to us and to all real Corkonians it was always Pana. Just inside Woolworths' door was a high mahogany sweet counter laden with good quality sweets: Malt Toffees, Cleeves' Everlasting Toffees, Bon Bons, Turkish Delight, Clarnico Murrays' and many other varieties. The main attraction for us was the section occupied by the broken Fry's Cream Chocolate bars which were on sale at half-price.

Watches and clocks took up another counter in this shop which to us was fairyland itself. On another counter hundreds of shiny metal-rimmed glasses were displayed. A piece of newsprint with letters in various sizes was encased in a frame beside them, and all the customers were required to do was to try the glasses on pair by pair until they came upon a pair which best enabled them to read the words. Needless to say at one shilling and sixpence a pair those spectacles were in great demand. Their suitability, however, was open to question but poor people cannot be choosers.

Everything one could possibly need for the home was available in Woolworth's, including mousetraps, hammers, scissors, cutlery and even rubber stoppers for kitchen sinks. The young girls working at the mousetrap counter always had a wooden spoon at their disposal with which to spring any traps that some young blackguard might have secretly set in the hope of catching the girls' fingers. Shortly before Mam was married she bought a picture there for sixpence and had a rosewood frame put on it which set her back twelve shillings and sixpence, a costly item at the time. It portrayed the Blessed Virgin clothed in an olive green mantle and the Child Jesus in a cream-coloured garment. The sadness in the Blessed Virgin's eyes seemed to foretell the fate that later befell the Holy Child on Calvary. That picture, so big that it almost took up one wall of our bedroom, played a large part in my young life because whenever I stole a fistful of sugar or was guilty of some other such little misdemeanour I fancied that the Blessed Virgin's eyes followed me around the room as if to remind me continuously of my guilt.

The large drapery shops in Cork were far beyond Mam's financial capabilities but because of her involvement in dressmaking she always found that a visit during sales time was well worth while. Dowden's in Patrick Street was perhaps the poshest of them all and only the well-off people dealt there. As a mark of its status the assistants all wore a type of morning-suit. Now and again Mam might go there in search of a piece of exotic lace to trim a First Communion or Confirmation dress for one of her customers. The Munster Arcade was another beautiful shop where materials from different parts of the world were stocked almost from floor to ceiling. Men's suitings from the woollen mills in Blarney, Douglas and Dripsey were on display beside Harris Scottish tweed, while Paisley cottons vied with the cottons and poplins from Ireland. There was always a dazzling array of silks from the Far East, but for Mam the real attraction was the remnants of material which were on sale at clearance prices.

As in many of the other highclass shops the Munster Arcade staff were extremely courteous to all customers, and I still cherish the sight of Gran dressed in her black shawl being given a chair to sit on by a floorwalker in morning-suit while she waited to be served. When having made a purchase you handed the assistant the money he or she put it into a small canister, pulled a lever and the canister whizzed along a wire overhead and into the office. The receipt and change were returned from the office on another wire and the assistant handed them to the customer.

Mannix and Culhane's in Washington Street, which is one of the few survivors from my childhood days, always had a clearance basket outside their door, and Mam, who had a passion for hats, could buy a nice one for sixpence. Moynihan's of Winthrop Street stocked great bargains at sales time and remnants of the finest materials were available at greatly reduced prices. Mam's cupboard was forever full of ruby red, bottle green and royal blue pieces of velvet from which she could run up a dress for one of us girls and any piece left over she put on the collars of our coats to give them a look of class.

Balls of Temptation

The street commonly known as the Coal Quay is in fact Cornmarket Street. The official Coal Quay, as one would expect, runs beside the River Lee from the bottom of Cornmarket Street to the present-day car-park forty or fifty yards to the east. However since Cornmarket Street has been known to generations of Cork people as the Coal Quay I may as well follow the accepted practice and give it its usual name.

Although the Coal Quay today is only a pale shadow of what it once was it is still the dearest place of all to the people of the city, particularly to the women. It has been a lifeline to them down the years. No true Corkwoman would let a morning pass – Sunday was the only exception – without a visit to her beloved open-air market. It helped to break the monotony of their lives as it enabled them to meet their friends with whom perhaps they had worked many years before, have a chinwag, read their husbands and mind one another's children. It enabled them to savour the wit of the dealing women who carried on their business there and also provided them with the welcome opportunity of securing bargains in old clothes, food, furniture, indeed almost everything from a needle to an anchor.

From ten o'clock in the morning one could see droves of women converging on the Coal Quay, many of them with babies in prams while the older children hung on to the handles of the prams. Those from the south side of the city would come in through Castle Street while the people of the Northside would approach from Kyle Street. My grandmother and mother initiated me into life on the Coal Quay at a very early age. It was bred into me. Not surprisingly therefore I still love to walk downtown every day through the North Main Street into the Coal Quay, visit the old secondhand shops there, go down Patrick Street and then having completed the ritual retrace my steps back home.

On entering the top of the Coal Quay in those far-off days one would suddenly behold a solid mass of people. City people, country people and the travelling community all mingled together, and then of course there were the dealers. Chat, gossip and banter filled the air. Each group could be identified by their dress or by the way they wore their hair. The city woman had her hair coiled around in loops at the nape of her neck whereas the country woman had hers pinned into a bun on the crown of her head. The country woman favoured a long dark coat while now and then you might see one of them with the traditional hooded cloak drooping from her shoulders. However the most colourful was the travelling woman for she always wore the rocky-o shawl which was a lovely fawn colour with a zig-zag border of brown all around the end. That shawl stood out in contrast to the plain black one of the city woman. You couldn't but admire the travelling women's gait as they strutted proudly as a peacock from dealer to dealer examining the various items on sale. Meanwhile their husbands leaned over the shafts of their carts which were always parked just below the Bridewell Garda Station. These men kept a careful eye on proceedings as their piebald horses stamped their feet impatiently on the ground waiting like their men for the women to complete their purchases and head back for the caravans or tents which were home to them on the outskirts of the city. Those tents were known as bender tents because they were made by bending long saplings into a semicircle and sticking both ends into the ground. Oilskins would then be spread over those saplings to keep out the rain. In those days neither the dealers nor anybody else could find fault with the travelling people. They were extremely honourable and though they drove a hard bargain their money was as good as anyone else's.

The country people's parking spot was on the blind or east side of the street in front of what was then Musgrave's wholesale premises. Their horses and butts were far more sedate than those of the travelling community. To us they were country people but in actual fact they were mainly market gardeners who lived and worked in areas which have now become built up and form part of the city, Pouladuff, Hangdog Road, Blackrock and other places mostly on the south side of the river where the soil was limey and suitable for growing vegetables. They also came from places farther afield such as Ballincollig, Carrigaline and Minane Bridge. Market days were Tuesdays, Thursdays and Saturdays and on those mornings the market gardeners, often accompanied by their wives, left their homes at the crack of dawn so as to reach the city in time to sell their produce. Little wonder then that they often appeared exhausted as they waited by their carts with varying degrees of patience for their womenfolk to return after completing the necessary shopping.

In early summer Thursday was the busiest day because that was when the early potato growers from Ballycotton arrived with their horse-loads of British Queens. They would have left home at one or two o'clock in the morning to complete the journey of well over twenty miles sufficiently early. Some farmers' wives brought eggs and chickens and country butter to sell to certain shopkeepers in the city. Women from the Blarney and Coachford area travelled to Cork on the train familiarly known as the Muskerry Tram, and were usually able to sell everything they had as soon as they alighted from the train at the station which was just west of where Jurys Hotel now stands.

The Muskerry Tram was renowned for its slowness. It ran along the side of the Carrigrohane Straight Road and was once involved in a famous crash with a steamroller which Cork people would have you believe occurred as the steamroller overtook it. A story is told of a postman who was delivering letters on foot on the Straight Road – postmen were not allowed to use bicycles in those days. Walking along westwards he caught up with the train.

'Hop up there, John,' said the driver, 'and we'll give you a lift.'

'Ah, no thanks, Mick,' said the postman. 'I'm in a hurry this morning.'

Each Coal Quay dealer had her own pitch on the side of the street. A small number of them had timber huts, others had trestles, but the majority of them just had spaces of their own and did their dealing off the ground. The majority were in the business of selling old clothes. As soon as one of them arrived with her bag, which she brought along on her back or in a child's pram, a crowd would gather around her eagerly waiting for her to untie the bag and display her wares. The would-be purchasers jostled for a vantage point to get the best possible view as the dealer held up each garment for inspection.

'Who will give me two bob for this lovely shirt?' she would say, not really expecting anyone to do so.

Nobody would budge. She would hold up the shirt again, turning it round for all to see and all the time extolling its quality and value. Then she would hand it to the nearest customer and ask her to feel the quality.

'Is there anyone of ye who will give me one and six for it?' Still nobody would budge.

'What in the name of God is wrong with ye all this morning? Will someone give me a bob for it?'

Of course it was all a game and the players on both sides were old hands at it. The onlookers were well able to judge her bottom price, and just as she, as it were, was about to withdraw the garment from sale by placing it on the reject pile on the ground some woman who needed a shirt for her better half would stretch out her hand, examine the shirt well and then hand over her shilling.

All secondhand clothes dealers were very particular as to whom they sold the first article. This was due to a certain superstition, a belief on their part that there were certain customers who brought luck with them and if they were to sell the first article to one of those customers then they would prosper that day. These customers who were thought to bring luck were said by the dealers to have a good hansel which meant a good day's business and a possible clearance of all the articles on sale. The dealers were very easy on a woman with a good hansel and would usually let her have the article at a reduced price. When the money was handed over she would spit on it for luck before putting it for safe-keeping in the specially made pocket of her apron.

Certain women were considered to have a bad hansel. On one occasion which I vividly remember I witnessed a dealer bluntly refusing to sell her first article to a woman whom she knew quite well.

'No, Mam,' she said. 'I'm not selling it to you, not if you were to give twice the price for it. You have bad hansel and I wouldn't have an hour's luck for the day if I took your money.'

Once the dealer had got good hansel it was open to all and sundry to purchase whatever articles they required. Thank goodness my mother had good hansel and I often noticed that when a dealer was about to open her bundle and commence selling she would say to my mother: 'Mrs Mac, would you have a lop on you there for hansel?'

The Cork term for a penny was a 'lop'. My mother would hand her a penny, and the penny would come back to her ten-fold if she bought off that dealer. There was one dealer whose tongue was always a bit on the acidy side. She never called out her prices but just held the various garments up for inspection, and waited for someone to make her a bid. She was considered to be on the expensive side but in fairness she sold good quality clothes. The city women were wise to her and rarely walked into her trap, but not so the country women. One day a country woman persisted in questioning her on the price of each article which she held up for inspection. Finally the dealer became exasperated and said, 'If I were you, Mam, I'd go away back to the country before I'd buy something.'

On another occasion I saw a country woman buying a jumper from her.

'Can I take it over to himself to see if I can buy it?' she asked.

Permission was duly granted and when she traipsed over to consult with her husband the dealer shouted out for all to hear: 'Will ye look at the pair of them! Will he or won't he let her buy it? I'd have a farm bought and sold again while I'm waiting to know will he let her give me one and six for a jumper.'

Her husband did in fact agree to let her buy the jumper and luckily so because it avoided her having abuse heaped on her.

The dealers had many admirable qualities. If a customer had an article in her hand and was bargaining with one of them and another woman was to cut in before the price was agreed and offered to buy it, the second woman would be curtly told: 'No, Mam, I wouldn't sell it to you out of that woman's hand, not even if you were to give me more money for it.' The second woman's bid would not be entertained until the first had clearly indicated that she was no longer interested. In such a situation you had to watch your step, and wait until the woman who had the article in her hand left it down and departed the scene before attempting to purchase it. The banter between dealer and customer was always an attraction. A dealer would hold up a night-dress and shout out: 'Anyone here for the Erinville?' The Erinville was a well-known maternity hospital.

Then she would survey the crowd around her and address one of them: 'Maggie, what about you? Your baby is walking around now, isn't he? Your time must be coming. You look a bit peaky.'

Then Maggie unfazed would laugh as she retorted: 'Keep your bad eye off me, will you? You might want it yourself before long, so if I were you I'd keep it. Anyway the last time you said that to me I really did land in the Erinville.'

Surveying the crowd gathered around her the dealer would spot another woman with a happy disposition and say: 'Peggie, wait till you see what I have for your Joe this morning.'

Rummaging through the clothes she would pull out a

man's jacket: 'This should fit him down to the ground. 'Twas made for him, I tell you, and I'll give it to you for just five bob. And I have the pants of it here too.'

A bob was of course the Cork word for a shilling.

'He'd be a right Dickie Dasher if he walked out in that,' the dealer would continue.

She'd then hold up the jacket and pants for inspection. Peggie would answer to everybody's amusement: 'Is it the way you want him to be stolen on me or what? Sure if he walked down Pana in that rig-out I'd never see him again.'

'There's no harm in thinking it, Peggie, I suppose. But I think you'd want to pin a ten-pound note on the lapel before anyone would steal Joe on you.'

Another dealer would take a dress from the pile and hold it aloft: 'Who'll give me a shilling for this dress. Look at it. 'Tis spanking new. Just feel the quality of it.'

No one in the crowd would take the bait. Then she would start again: 'What in the name of God is wrong with ye all this morning? Mary girl, 'tis about your size and God knows 'tis your colour too.'

'Yerrah,' Mary would reply, 'if my fellow saw me in that he'd think I was gone off me game. 'Tis much too loud for me.'

'Not at all, girl. Sure you'd be all style.'

'Yeah, I'd be all style and Johnnie idle.'

The women gathered around would be all smiles by now, and the dealer would continue her sales talk.

'Who'll give me ninepence for the lovely dress? Is there anyone who'll give me a tanner for it?'

Then as she was about to place it down on the ground and go on to the next article some woman who was interested would hand her a tanner, that is sixpence.

At the top of the Coal Quay near Castle Street corner the onion-dealer had her stand. She was a tiny olive-skinned doll-like woman who sold nothing but onions. As you approached she would hold out her hands full of onions.

'Hold up yer bib, Mam,' she would say, 'and I'll throw

them in for just two pence. Look at them, Mam, the finest of Spanish onions.'

Who minded if those same onions were grown out in Friars' Walk, as indeed they probably were? This black-shawled little woman's memory has been preserved for many future generations of Cork people because the loveable and talented stone sculptor Séamus Murphy, a bed in heaven to him, carved her figure with her two hands full of onions and that figure is now located in Bishop Lucey Park within a stone's throw of the spot where for many years she eked out a living.

Further down the street was a woman who sold apples. One morning she was sitting on a doorstep calling out for anyone interested: 'A penny each the apples! A penny each the apples!' Then out of the corner of her eye she espied a well-dressed lady walking along the footpath in her direction. She correctly took her to be an American visitor. Immediately she became slightly more specific: 'Two pence each the lovely American apples!' The American lady, seeing the humour and admiring the inventiveness of the dealing woman, bought some.

Near the little onion-woman was another who sold stale, or as Cork people would say, cold bread at half the normal price, and because of the difficult circumstances in which many families found themselves in those days she did quite a good business. Her pitch was the corner of Basket Lane, so called because there was a firm there which made cane baskets of every size and shape.

Close by was the veal-man, one of the few men who plied their trade there. He had a big oval basket from the top of which canes jutted out all around like the spokes of a wheel. From each of these canes hung a leg of veal. His cry was: 'Two and eightpence for a whole leg of veal! Think of it, a whole week's eating for two and eight!' But my mother was not impressed by his sales-talk and would say to whoever was with her: 'Will you take one look at the way the skin is bulging out from the flesh. Them farmers, sure you couldn't be up to them!

I'm sure they pump it up with a bicycle pump to make it look bigger before they sell it.'

Need I say we never had veal in the house!

The man who sold second-hand books from an old table was overshadowed by all the vegetable dealers around him.

'Come over here to me, Mam,' you would hear them cry, 'and buy some of me fine cabbages. Or maybe you might like a turnip or some lovely fresh parsnips. Hold up your bib there and I'll throw them in for you.'

Most women never brought a basket with them when shopping. They didn't need one because under their shawls they wore a butcher-blue spotlessly clean apron or bib tied around the waist. That apron was the receptacle for everything they bought. No one knew what it contained and having completed their purchases they would gather up the end of the apron to the waist with one hand thus leaving the other hand free to manage the shawl. Hence the saying 'Hold up yer bib.' The potato sellers were the greatest exaggerators of all. Their produce was on display on a rather high table with three or four boiled potatoes on an enamel plate to entice purchasers. The skins of those potatoes would be bursting open exposing the white floury flesh inside. Then you would hear the voice ringing out: 'Another donkey-load for a tanner, Mam. Come over to me and I'll have great luck for the day from your hansel. Look at them, Mam, balls of temptation!'

The compliment about the good hansel was designed to coax the would-be purchaser, and if she succumbed to the flattery and decided to buy the dealer would scoop up some potatoes with another enamel plate and heave them into the woman's apron. That plateful piled high was the donkey-load. It was not unusual, however, for a woman to find that on boiling the potatoes at home they were not as floury as those they had seen on display on the enamel plate.

'Balls of temptation how are you!' I heard one disappointed woman remark. 'That one put them into a tea-towel and squeeze the daylights out of them. That's how she got them to break open.'

My family were great customers of the blonde button-dealer who always had on her waist-high trestle ribbons of every hue, cards of bias binding, velvet braids for trimming homemade garments, cards of elastic which she sold by the yard and job-lot bales of cloth. She never had to resort to the use of a measuring tape to cut a yard of material. She simply held the end of the piece of cloth at the middle of her chest with one hand and then ran her other hand along the edge of the cloth until it was completely outstretched at right angles to her body. The distance between was a yard, but she had a heavy hand when cutting the cloth and always added on a tilly, a bit extra. The yard of elastic she measured differently. That was the equivalent of eight times the distance of the back of her middle finger from the tip of the nail to the knuckle.

At her feet beside the trestle she had a tea chest which was always filled to the brim with sample cards of buttons of the type used by commercial travellers as they went from shop to shop selling their wares. It was for these buttons and not the other items which she sold that we best remember this dealer. That is why she was always known to us and indeed to everyone else as the button-woman. Each card had a gross of buttons stitched on to it, and every shade under the sun was represented, blue, green, red, pink, yellow and brown, as well as black and white. They winked up invitingly at the customer. 'Twopence a gross of buttons', the dealer would call out.

The thought struck my mother one day that if she could find six cards of identical buttons she would have a complete set for every dress and coat she would make for us children for many years to come, so she rummaged through the tea-chest until she found six identical cards, and for twelve pence, or five pence in today's money, she took home eight hundred and sixty-four buttons. They came in extremely handy when the time arrived for her to throw open her door and take in sewing-work for the neighbours. As we grew up and became interested in card-playing we used some of these buttons in lieu of money, and if we lost the markers for our Ludo game all we had to do was to open Mam's button-box, find four buttons of the same colour and we were in business again.

I remember Mam falling in love with a delicate coffee-set made of fine bone china, a beautiful piece of crockery indeed. It was very foreign looking to her eye and even though one or two pieces were missing she wasn't perturbed. After all the set was only for ornamental purposes because as for coffee neither ourselves nor any of the neighbours would drink the stuff. We were strictly tea and cocoa drinkers. As we were admiring the various pieces after she brought the set home we noticed that the tip of the jug had been very delicately stitched, and having made enquiries shortly afterwards we found out that Mayne's shop in Patrick Street, which is now part of Dunnes Stores, provided a repair service for fine china by stitching. In those days too some of the travelling people were skilled in stitching fine china.

Fish, including sprats, mackerel, conger eels and herring were also sold from stalls in the Coal Quay. I recall a woman who sold what she called rock salmon, but many people suspected that it was mullet taken from the Lee at at North Gate Bridge and on which she had conferred a fancy name, so they gave her stall a wide berth. Many of the small shops which lined the western side of the Coal Quay carried on a thriving business selling an array of household furniture, sewing machines, prams, books, gramophones and gramophone records, all second-hand, of course.

St Peter's Meat Market, which stretched indoors from the Coal Quay right across to the North Main Street and is now a furniture and carpet shop, contained several stalls where one could buy all sorts of pig's meat, beef and mutton. The butchers there were known as the Randy Butchers, not because they themselves were possessed of any extra sexual drive but because of the kind of meat which they sold. It was very cheap and not of the best quality. In fact it was generally accepted that they often passed off goat-meat for mutton to customers who were gullible enough to buy it, and the goat, in the minds of Cork people at any rate, is one of the most fertile animals known to man. This accounted for the rather unflattering nickname 'Randy'. One of these rogue butchers, whenever he succeeded in duping a customer, would boast to the fellow next to him: 'I sold her a bit of the angel with the whisker, Paddy McGinty's goat.'

To facilitate the country people who brought their produce into the city in the early hours of the morning the public houses were granted a special licence to open their doors at seven o'clock. Of course country people weren't the only ones to avail of the early opening. There was one dealer woman who did so regularly and long before it was time to start operating at her pitch she would be three sheets in the wind. Selling studs for the collars of men's shirts was her way of making a few shillings and most people in the Coal Quay knew when she had been overdiligent in slaking her thirst. Her repeated announcement: 'A penny each the ha'penny studs!' was the give-away. For some alcoholics also, who couldn't wait until normal opening hours, the pubs on the Coal Quay were a godsend.

There were two or three eating-houses – they were never called restaurants – which like the pubs opened at the dawn of the morning to cater for the country people. In any of those farmers could get a mug of tea and bread and butter, with perhaps a bit of black pudding or a fry. Sometimes down-and-outs dropped in hoping to benefit from farmers' generosity. Rough eating, maybe, but the prices were reasonable. The doors were usually wide open as the customers were well accustomed to God's fresh air, and you could look in the door and see the plain wooden tables covered with oilcloth usually patterned in red and white. After the farmers departed for home some of the down-and-outs of the city would go in for a mug of tea and a thick chunk of bread, usually known to Cork people as a 'baat' of bread. None of your fancy slices for them. Quantity not quality was of the essence.

Kattie Barry's sheebeen was by far the most famous of all the Coal Quay institutions. It was located on the eastern side of the street. Kattie was a beautiful woman in her day, tall stately and erect. She never opened the premises until the public houses had closed for the night. It was anything but posh, a sort of rundown shop, and though some people who never went inside the door liked to give the impression that it was a house of somewhat ill-repute it certainly was not so. There patrons could buy wine, admittedly a very cheap kind, and sometimes bottles of beer as well, but though she never had a licence to sell drink the guards whose barracks were across the street turned a blind eye and allowed her to carry on. Some of her customers were what one might describe as run-of-the-mill drinkers. Some of them were judges or solicitors or students mostly from the Medical Faculty in UCC. Many were actors, particularly those appearing in the Opera House nearby, while others might be visitors to Cork whose hosts would like them to see and experience the various aspects of life in the city. Kattie's was almost akin to a place of pilgrimage. There was no such thing as a counter nor indeed were there any chairs, only an odd stool. Patrons sat on the steps of the stairs and anywhere and everywhere around the floor while Kattie herself was busily engaged boiling crubeens in a huge tin bath at the back of the premises. Some of the patrons would be crawsick having consumed too much drink and delighted in sucking the fat crubeens so expertly boiled by the hostess herself. All the time great conversation and wit abounded.

The Coal Quay lost its greatest character and most famous daughter with the passing of Kattie Barry. Even today people recall her name with fondness and indeed with much admiration, aware as they are that she made a unique contribution to the culture and lore of their city. No one ever heard a bad word being said about Kattie.

On Saturday mornings life on the Coal Quay took on an added dimension with the appearance of the street artists to entertain the people. There was one fellow who used to sit on a chair and contort his body into the shape of a monkey. Another would lie on a board of nails and a bed of broken glass. In silent awe we watched him get up and waited to see the lacerations on his back but to our amazement there never were any, just a small number of little red marks, and we wondered what manner of man was he. However our favourite entertainer was a middle-aged woman known to all as Banjo Annie. She sang to her own not always note-perfect accompaniment. 'Two Little Girls in Blue' was her favourite song.

The dealers of the Coal Quay were the salt of the earth. They knew practically all their customers, and they knew their circumstances also. They were never hard on the poor. Rather would they go out of their way to help them. They had a special admiration for women who struggled hard to bring up their families, especially the woman who had lost her husband, and ensured that she got whatever bargains were going. They would put the best of fruit aside for her and throw one or two extra oranges into her bib. I remember especially the banana-woman who was extremely generous to my mother and to many others as well. She would give you six bananas for a shilling. We just loved bananas as indeed we did the oranges, because those were the immediate postwar years and fruit was a novelty since we never could get any fruit during the war. Sometimes you would find two bananas in one skin and my mother called those 'batons'. However, the dealers would not be as easy on the country women whom they found to be given to haggling and questioning the price of everything. Consequently when a country woman came along the dealer would ask twice the price which she hoped to get eventually and then come down gradually, leaving the country-woman under the impression that she was in fact getting a bargain.

Whether you were from the country or the city you had to bargain with the dealers. In fact they expected that. If one of them asked five shillings for a garment you held it up, examined it thoroughly as it were, and then offered a half-crown, which was half the asking price. Some of the dealers might be at daggers drawn with those trading beside them because of alleged encroaching on pitches or maybe simply because they were neighbours and didn't get on very well, but on the Coal Quay business was business, they forgot their differences for the time being and supported one another whenever necessary. So one of them might say to the dealer next to her, enemies though they were: 'Biddy, she's offering me a half-crown for this jumper, and don't you know I paid that much for it meself.'

'You did, girl,' Biddy would reply.

More than likely the bargain would be struck at a price somewhere in between but if one wasn't wise to the dealers' way of doing business and paid the asking price the dealers saw nothing wrong in that. If you were a fool you paid for being a fool.

Clothes-dealers always finished business by half-past twelve or one o'clock even if they hadn't disposed of all their goods by that time. The only people doing business in the afternoons were the shopkeepers and those with stalls who sold different kinds of ware, sugar bowls, knives, forks and the like. The clothes-dealers always availed of the afternoons to call, complete with go-cars, to big houses in Douglas, Montenotte and Blackrock to buy cast-offs. Some of the housewives from whom they might have been buying for years would send them cards telling them that they had a load of clothes to sell, while others might meet them in town and make arrangements for them to call to their homes a day or two later. The dealers never washed those clothes before selling them on the Coal Quay and indeed they could not in fairness be expected to do so considering the small profit which they made. However the women who in turn bought the clothes from the dealers washed them thoroughly with carbolic soap, not the small bars but the big ones which were extra strong. Then they altered them to fit the children. They would never think of putting them on their children unwashed because of their fear of tuberculosis, or consumption as they called it, which was rampant at the time.

While the dealers were out trying to earn a living the children looked after one another at home. As soon as the girl-child reached the age of eight she was trained in how to mind the younger ones and take over the running of the house until the mother returned. Being able to shoulder responsibility at such a young age must certainly have helped them in later years. The mothers worked hard and if they made money they used it to provide full and plenty for the family. I recall as a child coming home on the Youghal train one evening after a day at the seaside. There were dealer-women and their children in the carriage with us and when they saw that our food had run out they opened up a cloth in which they had a couple of cooked chickens, tore the breasts and legs and wings off with their hands and saw to it that none of us went without.

Chicken was a very common dish on the dealers' tables. Some of them often travelled by bus to Macroom on market days with bundles of clothes to sell to the people of the area. Having disposed of the clothes they would then use some of the money to buy chickens from the farmers. During the time of the Troubles the Black and Tans might board the bus on the way out but they rarely bothered the dealers. Coming back to Cork in the evening was a different story, however, particularly if the Black and Tans had suffered a reverse at the hands of the IRA. Their resultant bad humour would have been made worse by drinking bouts designed to drown their sorrows. On such occasions they could be quite obstreperous, and it was not unknown for them to demand from the dealers the money which they had made in Macroom. After one or two such bitter experiences the dealers were always able to outwit them by the simple device of stuffing the money up the chickens' backsides.

The dealers lived in tenements all over the centre of the city but particularly in the lanes and alleyways in the Marsh which coincides approximately with the area around the

63

Mercy Hospital and St Francis Church. Some also lived in tenements in the big houses in Moore Street, Paul Street and Kyle Street. The front doors of the tenement houses were never locked because of all the families living in them, and this proved a great boon to down-and-outs who could go in from the weather and spend the night sleeping on the stairs. Occupants of the tenements going to work early in the morning often had to pick their way down the stairs over sleeping bodies. A tenement in those houses usually consisted of a large room with a smaller one off it which served as a bedroom. Even in the unavoidably crowded conditions in which those with larger families lived the women kept beautiful homes, full of dainty old ornaments. These they picked up while buying clothes around the city and kept them to decorate their homes rather than sell them.

It is to the eternal credit of many of the dealers that as a result of their hard work on the Coal Quay in all sorts of weather their children benefited greatly. They insisted on their children going to school and paying attention to their lessons and any child who showed promise was helped in every possible way. It is no wonder then that some of those children became doctors and dentists or entered other professions far above their parents' station in life.

The Coal Quay dealers' husbands were not as much in the limelight as their wives but they were a tough breed and many of them drank heavily. Nevertheless they were always prepared to turn their hand to anything that would bring in a few shillings, such as working on the docks, furniture removal and fishing on the Lee. Some of them fished for herrings, sprats and mullet. Their wives sold the herring and sprats from their stalls but because mullet frequented the river wherever the sewers entered it nobody except chip-shop owners would buy them. Seemingly people who were customers of those shops either didn't know or didn't care what they were eating. Other men spent a good deal of time fishing for salmon off the bridges and used the stroke-hauling method, commonly known in Cork as 'strawcalling'. This was done with a large three-pronged hook and was of course illegal, but they had watch-outs at vantage points up and down the river-bank so as to avoid detection. They were expert practitioners, could spot a salmon far off, and once they hooked it they could haul it out in a flash with just a flick. They would then put the fish under their coats and walk nonchalantly away. They seldom left any marks on the fish, an odd time perhaps on the tail but rarely if ever on the rest of the body.

If the Coal Quay women possessed a great sense of community so too did their husbands who never hesitated to back the underdog. Never did they prove their mettle more than during the tailors' strike. At that time everybody depended on tailors and tailoresses for their new clothes. Many of them were also employed by the British Army and were paid what they considered a mere pittance for their work, so in exasperation but with great reluctance they went on strike. The government did its level best to break them and having failed it decided to bring in tailors from Germany to replace the locals. Immediately those tailors arrived the Coal Quay men took up the cause of their fellow-Corkmen. Together with many supporters from the Southside they came out on to the streets every night. The Coal Quay men came from the Northside on to Patrick Street where they were met by the Southsiders who would have come up across the bridges spanning the South Channel of the Lee. They would be baton-charged and beaten back down the Coal Quay but they would fight every inch of the way back to their tenement doors and up the stairs. Then their womenfolk would join the fray and rain down upon the heads of the police the under-bed vessels, preferably full, pots and any other suitable missile available. These activities continued every night until the strike was fixed satisfactorily and the German tailors were sent packing.

The Coal Quay husbands were great drinkers and scarcity of money was always a problem for them but sometimes their wives took pity on them. If a wife guessed that her husband had no money she would slip him the price of one or two pints. That was what one might call his admission fee. He would then go to the local pub where he would meet some friend of his who was, as they used to say, in the money. Free drink after free drink would be placed in front of him on the counter and his joy was complete. Then on his return home he would say to his wife: 'There's no doubt at all, girl, but you have a drunkard's hansel.' Proud was the man whose wife had that.

Sadly there are very few dealers left on the Coal Quay today. Theirs is a dying trade. The women of the present generation are not prepared to put up with the hardship which their mothers and grandmothers endured, and even if they were to continue the tradition they would almost certainly find themselves with few customers prepared to purchase second-hand clothes and alter and turn them in for their sons and daughters. In any case those sons and daughters are more pampered nowadays and wouldn't deign to be seen in such attire. So different are they and so fussy have they become that quite often when their mothers bring even something new home from the shops they refuse to wear it. Perhaps they are not altogether as poor as they would have us believe. Either that or they are constantly in debt.

JAMJARS & FOLLOWING-UPPERS

The cinemas – we always called them picture houses – played a great part in our lives. For the adults they were an escape, even though a shortlived one, from the tribulations and hardship of the world, and for the children who knew little about radio and absolutely nothing about television they represented the only amusement available other than the gramophone and whatever games they played.

The finest cinema in Ireland in my childhood days was the Savoy in Patrick Street. Diagonally across from it was the rather small Lee Cinema at the junction of Patrick Street and Winthrop Street while further up Patrick Street was the Pavilion, known to all and sundry as The Pav. There were two cinemas in MacCurtain Street, the Palace which is now the Everyman Theatre, and the Coliseum, the Col to us, down at the corner of MacCurtain Street and Clontarf Street. In Washington Street opposite St Augustine's Church was the Washington which was burnt down and later on rebuilt and renamed the Ritz. Some years later the present Capitol was built on a site occupied originally by Grant's Store which was the victim of a bad fire.

Fine and all as those cinemas were by far the most popular with us children was the Assembly Rooms on the South Mall, the reason being that it screened the best cowboy pictures in town and was more suited to our pockets. The cheapest part of the 'Assems' cost fourpence, a not inconsiderable sum to us, and there we would be seated crushed together on hard benches as we watched the singing cowboys Gene Autry and Roy Rodgers galloping across the screen. For us girls they were our favourite stars because they had an eye for the leading ladies. We loved the moment when they put their hands around female stars but the boys were not impressed and would stamp the ground with their feet and give them the 'razz', which was the Cork word for jeering. The boys' preference was for Charles Starrett, the Durango Kid, Johnny Mack Brown, Hopalong Cassidy and Tim Holt. The cowboys often had comic characters as pals on the films. Fuzzy Knight, Cannon Ball and Leon Errol usually filled that role and their presence added greatly to our enjoyment. Gabby Hayes was always Hopalong Cassidy's pal. As the cowboy was shooting all around him and killing all the baddies some of the boys would shout out: 'Hey, Slim, come in and take out the bodies!' Slim, a tall thin figure of a man as his nickname implied, worked in the Assems as an usher and whenever the roaring started or the boys became slightly unruly Slim would rush in and flash his torch along the seats in an effort, usually unsuccessful, to find the culprits. If the film broke down, as it sometimes did, pandemonium took over. Everyone present, boys and girls, clapped their hands, stamped their feet, hooted and whistled and shouted: 'We want our money back! We want our money back!' In spite of Slim's best endeavours the rumpus continued until the picture was restored.

The Imperial in Oliver Plunkett Street was the cheapest picture-house in the south side of the city. It was also one of the nearest to us. It certainly belied its name as it was impossible to imagine an establishment less imperial. Perhaps that is why it was never known by any name other than Miah's. The name Miah is a contraction of Jeremiah and the man from whom the cinema got its name was a gentle attendant who did his best to run the cinema and keep the queues in order. Queues there were aplenty, for apart from the cheap admission fee it was one of the last houses in Cork to screen the 'following-uppers'. They were serials which held a great attraction for children as each part ended with the heroine hanging on to a bush down the face of a cliff or tied firmly to a plank of wood with a circular saw approaching to cut her in half. Consequently children were eager to return to Miah's when the programme changed a few days or maybe a week later to witness the outcome of the poor heroine's predicament.

Miah's had a floor that sloped down to the screen, under

which there were gas-heaters where patrons could dry their coats if the weather was wet. Young children were accompanied by their older brothers and sisters, and if they wanted to go to the toilet, as young children often do at the most inappropriate times, their brothers and sisters were so engrossed that they would ignore their requests. When finally the picture ended and the lights came on the floor would be one large puddle especially towards the front.

Children were often accompanied by their mothers. It frequently occurred that these children, riveted to their seats by the programme, completely ignored full bladders and the need to go to the toilet lest they miss even a minute of the excitement. Then the main feature would follow, and if that involved any romance the women in turn would become so engrossed that they ignored the pleas of their offspring to accompany them to the toilet in case they missed the lovey-dovey parts. The result was inevitable, and the children uninterested in the film and uncomfortable in their wet clothes became more cranky by the minute. Then a mother in exasperation would catch hold of the fringe of her shawl by this time streeling in the wiggles on the floor, and a deft flick of that sodden shawl into the cheek or eye would with unerring aim silence the most obstreperous child. Another memorable feature of Miah's was its colony of fleas probably unequalled anywhere else. They assailed you the moment you entered. It was the place where it was said you went in a cripple and came out walking!

The first picture I ever saw was shown in Miah's. My father had shortly beforehand secured some work and was earning, so one day Mam gathered us all together and brought us down to Miah's. It was a Shirley Temple movie and in it she sang 'The Good Ship Lollipop'. We just loved it and from that on we fell hook, line and sinker for the silver screen. On our return home my graphic description of the film so aroused Gran's interest that out of the blue she announced: 'I'll take that child there to the pictures tomorrow.' We could scarcely believe our ears because Gran would not readily forfeit her afternoon nap for anything. Looking through the advertisements on the *Echo* she chose *The Lily of Killarney* which was being shown in the Lee Cinema. Before we entered the cinema next afternoon she brought me into Cudmore's Shop just across the street and bought me a packet of hard sweets called Fruitos, to keep me quiet I presume. Then she bought our tickets and we went in. Oh, the luxury of it compared to Miah's! A lovely plush seat for every patron and plenty of room. Soon after the film commenced I glanced sideways at Gran and in the darkness I could just see her towering over me. Being unaware that she should have tilted the seat forward to sit on it she was in fact perched high up on its edge. In spite of the obvious discomfort which she was bound to inflict on her posterior I refrained from pointing out her mistake because she never took too kindly to children correcting adults. The problem was however rectified by the woman sitting behind her whose view of the screen was seriously obstructed. That night Gran gave Granda, who had never seen a sound picture, a detailed and awe-filled account of her first cinematic experience.

'I can't fathom out how it was done,' she said. 'There was Frank Ryan the singer from County Waterford and the rest of them and they acting and talking. You'd swear it was really happening in front of your very eyes. And Frank Ryan, sure his singing was handsome!'

It seemed that she had been bitten by the cinema bug but once her initial curiosity had been satisfied her enthusiasm gradually waned. In any case she had too much respect for her money to spend it on something so transient as pictures and during the remainder of her life she saw only two more, *The Ten Commandments* and *Little Nellie Kelly*.

Mam was an avid cinema-goer and she loved to go to any film which featured such stars as Charles Boyer – she delighted in his soft foreign-sounding voice – Nelson Eddy, Stewart Granger, Errol Flynn and Tyrone Power. Many women had a soft spot for the latter two not only because of their dashing good looks but also they were reputed to have close Irish connections. The favourite female stars of Mam's time were Vivien Leigh, Ava Gardiner, Rita Hayworth, Maria Montez, Deanna Durbin who thrilled many a heart with her singing, and of course our very own Maureen O'Hara from Dublin.

The people of the north side of the city had two picture houses in their area, St Mary's Hall near the North Chapel where the admission fee was twopence, and the Lido in the heart of Blackpool. The Lido was a godsend to children or indeed anybody else who had difficulty in coming by the admission fee because during the war years jamjars were accepted there in lieu of money. These jars the management would in turn sell to jam manufacturers. There were two main sources of jamjars. One was the home. Every family ate a great deal of jam and when the jars were empty we washed them and put them aside until needed. On the other hand if we were short of jars or needed a few extra we would take a scove out to St Joseph's Cemetery on Tory Top Road.

Our journey would not have been inspired by any interest in the history of that cemetery. The land for it had been donated by Cork Corporation to Fr Matthew, the famous Tipperary-born Capuchin and Apostle of Temperance, as a burial ground for the poor, and a section of it is for some mysterious reason known as the Po-ground. That is where people who died on the streets or wherever else during the Famine were buried in mass graves. Our motive in going to the cemetery, sometimes referred to as the Botanic Gardens, was to look for jamjars in which people had placed flowers on the graves of their loved ones. We never interfered with the jars containing fresh flowers but confined our search to those which had obviously been forgotten about. They were usually full of slime but were easily washed. In due course we would bring them down to Henchion's shop in Barrack Street where one-pounders fetched a half-penny and two-pounders fetched a penny. That was because jars and glassware of any kind were in very short supply during the war.

If financial straits decreed that we could not afford to go to the pictures in the Southside we crossed over the North Gate Bridge and went to either the Lido or St Mary's Hall where I recall on one occasion the side-door being opened just before the end of the picture and a wandering donkey poking his way in and standing in the aisle before deciding to go out again. He mustn't have liked what he saw!

I cannot say who was the genius responsible for the following lines which children could often be heard reciting on their way to or from a picture-house:

I went to the pictures tomorrow;
I took a front seat in the back.
I fell from the pit to the gallery
And broke the front bone in me back.
I walked it home in a taxi;
I bought a plain currant bun.
I ate it and gave it to the driver
And that was the end of me fun.

LEESIDE AND SEASIDE

During fine summer weather Mam used to bring us up Gil-abbey Street to Canty's Field which was an open stretch of ground near the houses on Connaught Avenue. One part of the field was taken over by the boys who played hurling, football and rounders. The girls had their own area where they danced and skipped with ropes, all the while chanting various little rhymes. Another smaller area was reserved for the mothers who sat together on large stone seats chatting and at the same time keeping a sharp eye on their offspring. There was always a number of donkeys grazing there. These were owned by people living in the lanes and when there was no work for them to do their owners turned them out to graze in the field. It was from the antics of these animals that many Cork children learned one major fact of life, that mothers did not buy their babies from the maternity nurse.

On one side of the field were railings through which we could look down on the southern channel of the river Lee. A gap in the railings allowed the younger children to squeeze through and descend a narrow track down a face of rock to the river. This shortcut was quite dangerous and two young friends of mine broke their legs trying to negotiate it, but most of us were as sure-footed and agile as goats, particularly as we grew older. In that patch of river the boys learned to swim not with any of your modern buoyancy aids but with two empty paraffin-oil cans tied around their waists. The girls were less adventurous and confined their activities to paddling. When the tide ebbed both girls and boys could go walking in the mud of an inlet of water which ran through a lonely eerie glade down past the back of the palace of the Protestant Bishop of Cork, and search for the small flat fluke-like fish that frequented that particular spot. On one occasion the children lit a fire of paper and lollipop sticks to cook them heads and all but they proved inedible. In the autumn when the tide was out my pals and myself often crossed the river to the back of St Aloysius' School playing-field to feast on the luscious blackberries which grew in abundance there.

The arrival of Pipers Amusements in Cork for their annual season was an occasion of sheer bliss. My earliest recollection of the 'merries', as we called them, was when my mother brought me to see them in Deasy's Field. I was absolutely enthralled. Soon afterwards, however, when the housing estate now known as Greenmount Crescent was built on Deasy's Field the merries were transferred to an open space at the foot of Gilabbey Rock just off Donovan's Road. Mam knew how much my sisters and myself loved the merries but Gran frowned on what she saw as Mam's waste of good money in allowing us to become involved in such useless frivolity, so on Sunday afternoons as soon as Gran retired for her nap Mam would give us a few pence each and we would set off for Gilabbey Rock full of excitement and anticipation. Sometimes Mam accompanied us. A spin on the merry-go-round cost a penny, and how we loved those colourful horses with their heads held high, their flashing white teeth, their wild eyes and their black and grey tails flowing gracefully behind. Up and down they went in stately movement as we screamed with delight. The bravest amongst us held the reins with both hands, scorning the use of the safety wooden pole. The noise was deafening as the hit songs of the day blared out repeatedly from the loudspeakers. The accents of the good-looking women in charge of the stalls sounded strange to our young ears as they cajoled the crowd into purchasing tickets in the draws for half-sets of ware, enamel dishes, clocks, vases, sets of cutlery and statues of the Sacred Heart, the Blessed Virgin and all the other saints that were on exhibition.

Scarce and all though money was we nevertheless tried to keep a few pence to gamble on the roulette table. The man in charge of the table was rather stately-looking and of ample proportions, always impeccably dressed in a grey pin-striped suit with matching waistcoat across which stretched a heavy silver chain. The chain was attached to a large watch which he took out of his pocket now and again to check the time. As we crowded around the wheel we were as engrossed in the action as any gambler in Las Vegas. Then with booming voice the man would exhort the onlookers to put their hands in their pockets and have a gamble: 'Place your bets now please. Evens the black, two to one the red, five to one the blue, eight to one the yellow and twenty to one the crown, harp and anchor.'

Mam's favourite colour was the yellow and I often prayed that the silver ball which raced around the table would stop on the yellow because she would then give me a penny or two from her winnings. Some of the boys, hoping not to be detected, would delay placing their penny on a colour until the ball began to slow down but the eagle eye of the big man always saw them, and he promptly rapped their knuckles with the long stick which he used to gather in the pennies. Whenever I struck an unlucky patch and my money ran out – an occurrence far too common for my liking – there was nothing I liked better than to sit with my friends on the steps of the beautiful square Vardo caravans which were home to the people who ran the merries, and peep in at all the silvery and glittery ornaments inside. The owners never attempted to move us away, probably because they realised that we were up to no harm. I was so totally enraptured by those spotless caravans and their contents that had I the opportunity I would have gladly left my mother, father and relations to join the merries.

A regular feature of city life in those long lost days, and one which I now miss greatly, was the bands. The two best known to us were brass and reed bands, the Barrack Street Band, always referred to as the Barracka, and the Butter Exchange Band, which was never known as anything but the Buttera. Cork people always had a penchant for adding on an 'a' to the names of things or people held in affection by them. The flimsiest event was sufficient excuse for the bands to appear on our streets, and whenever they were heard approaching every door was flung open and the women and children rushed out to see the musicians all decked out in their caps, woollen coats and trousers with stripes down the legs.

When the bands passed by the women and children joined in behind to follow them wherever they went. The mothers might soon give up but the children continued on, lured by the rousing music and the sense of occasion. However there was no need for the mothers to worry about their offspring even when they were late returning as there was never a question of their being harmed. Sometimes a mother might have to put on her coat and follow the general direction the band had taken until she met the children perhaps lost or on their way home exhausted. Even on the hottest days the bands wore their heavy uniforms and how they survived the heat when playing at summer events only they themselves knew.

The Corpus Christi procession was a case in point even though that big occasion was sometimes marred by bad weather. Having played a succession of hymns on their way down to the centre of the city and having stood in the heat all through the sermon and Benediction on the Grand Parade they would then face for home covered in beads of perspiration and gasping from the thirst. By the time they reached the bottom of Barrack Street they had forgotten the hymns and reverted to some rousing tunes which they played with renewed gusto. The moment they caught sight of the Brown Derby Pub the thought of a few frothy pints and the anticipated slaking of their thirst enabled them to finish with a vigour the like of which they hadn't displayed all day. On the occasion of the funeral of the late and respected Bishop Cornelius Lucey in September 1982 some bands attended and played suitably sad and plaintive music. After the funeral, I am told, one of the bands was coming down Shandon Street and, happy in the knowledge that they had done their duty, they finished the piece of sacred music which they were playing and suddenly burst into a dashing rendering of 'When the Saints Come Marching In'. The sad part was over, the mood changed and they were bound for their local watering-place.

In spite of my affection for the brass-and-reed bands I much preferred the pipe-bands. St Finbarr's and the Volunteers' Band were the ones I knew best of all. There was something special about the beat of the big drum, the skirl of the pipes and the swirl of the kilts, so much so that I felt I would follow them to hell and back.

The men in our community had a special Sunday ritual. They got up fairly late and then the cut-throat razor made from cold blue steel, or maybe the Mac's Smile three-hole blade was pressed into service giving them skin like that of a baby. If the razor slipped or a pimple was nicked they would tear the tiniest piece of the *Echo*, dampen it with their tongue and apply it to the cut to stem the blood. After fulfilling its task the paper was removed. Then having eaten breakfast they left home all spruced up in their Sunday clothes and polished shoes to attend twelve o'clock Mass in the Lough Chapel. After Mass they immediately headed for the local pub with its sawdust-covered floor. Sometimes they had to wait outside for the doors to open. A half-crown would buy them three pints of porter, the amount needed, they maintained, to give them an appetite for their dinner. Then there was the inevitable game of cards. One Sunday a poor unfortunate man, after the pint he had ordered was placed in front of him, found to his horror that he had mistakenly put his half-crown on the collection plate in the Chapel and now had only his usual subscription of one penny in his pocket. Leaving his pint on the counter he ran as fast as his bockety legs could carry him back to the sacristy. Panting he said to the clerk: 'Will you look through the collection and give me back the half-crown I put on the plate instead of a penny.' The clerk, not renowned for his patience, bluntly told him to clear off out of his sight, so the poor man had to go on tick on Miss O's book rather earlier than he expected that week.

Around half-past two the men would emerge from the pub fortified by the black stuff, wipe the froth off their mouth with the backs of their hands and return home to a fine feed of meat, cabbage and potatoes. Then they retired to bed for a snooze, or perhaps the younger ones amongst them might go to a match or a game of bowls. Later that night, finances permitting, they would sally forth again to the watering hole.

It is obvious therefore that Sunday was a day when the men relaxed and enjoyed one another's convivial company. Small wonder then that they detested the thought of the children's annual pilgrimage to the seaside in Youghal and the hustle and bustle which it entailed. Some of them, including my father, refused point blank to accompany their wives and children on the trip, while others went along only because they perceived that it would be unfair of them to leave to the women the task of lifting the heavy old-fashioned prams into and out of the luggage compartments of the train. Mothers were firmly of the conviction that the salt air at the seaside was of immense benefit to children's health and consequently they would do their utmost to make the trip even if only on one Sunday in the year. Any family whose father was earning always set aside the Sunday of the August Bank Holiday weekend for Youghal, whereas the family whose father was out of work would go there on whatever Sunday they were able to scrape up the money to buy little extras such as biscuits, bananas and apples. If the mother succeeded in inveigling her husband to go she would bring along some cooked meat to assuage his hunger and hopefully his grumpiness.

Our own excursion was always planned well in advance downstairs around Gran's kitchen fire. Even if the Sunday was pelting rain out of the heavens we would still venture forth on that day because there wasn't the faintest hope that Mam could afford to buy the extras for us a second time. After early Mass dozens of families set out on foot for the station, every child's face scrubbed clean and shiny, the girls resplendent in coloured cotton frocks, the boys in short trousers and sporting new haircuts, the smaller children hanging on to the handle of the pram which contained the baby who was scarcely visible behind a mound of bags of food and the coats which might be required before the day was out. We all trotted along in our white rubber dollies which we had freshened up with a whitener made from a white powder mixed with water. When dry that mixture rose up in the air in the form of a white dust as we bounced joyfully along the pavements. This would not have occurred had we treated our rubber dollies with the proprietary Blanco which came in a box. You placed a round block of it on a saucer. A little pot-hole, as it were, on the top of the block enabled you to pour a drop of water into it. You got a piece of rag, rubbed it against the dampened Blanco and spread it on your rubber dollies which you then put out on the window-sill to dry. Blanco however cost money and our family used the home-made whitening instead because it was much cheaper.

The streets approaching the station were one mass of humanity and prams of all types and descriptions, with the people from the North Side wending their way along MacCurtain Street, those from Mayfield and Dillon's Cross pouring down Summerhill and the Southsiders crossing northwards over Patrick's Bridge and Clontarf Bridge. Then there was the scramble outside the ticket-office, the subsequent frantic efforts of parents to line up their children at the ticket-gate and all the time the din and the clamour. Only rarely were tickets bought for the children who were, as we used to say, ducked down. Because of the crush going through the gate the ticket collector would ignore most of the children, but if a mother had four or five children she would stand back and wait for a woman going past with no children. Then she would whisper to one of her own: 'Hang on to her coat there and pretend you're with her, but the minute you get past the collector let go and wait for me.' All credit to the collectors for they realised only too well the plight of mothers with large families and they rarely if ever ordered one of them back to buy extra tickets.

In due course everybody would get through and board the train after the prams had been loaded into the luggage coach. Every seat was taken up by adults with the children sitting on the floor and the babies up in someone's arms. As the train steamed out of the station the children would begin to chant:

> We all went down to Youghal;
> We let the baby fall.
> Me mother came out
> And gave us a clout
> And turned us into a bottle of stout.

That would be followed by another ditty:

> The day that we all went down to Youghal
> We had plenty there to ate for one and all.
> There was bread and hairy mate
> And lashings there to ate
> On the day that we all went down to Youghal.

There was another short ditty handed down to us children by previous generations:

> Goodbye Andy.
> Goodbye all.
> Goodbye Andy.
> We're all going down to Youghal.

That was a little tribute to a man who was Lord Mayor of Cork many years ago. He was instrumental in getting a free annual excursion to Youghal for the children of the poverty-stricken of the city. Their mothers would be at the station to see the children off and before boarding the train each child was given a currant bun which was supposed to do them for the day. It so happened on one of those excursions that a child who was leaning out the window of the train as it sped along eastwards let her bun fall on the track. The child became hysterical at the loss of her prized possession and at the instigation of some of the children she pulled the communication cord. The loss of a bun would in the eyes of the railway authorities certainly not justify such an action under normal circumstances but in this instance circumstances were not normal and the guard walked back along the line and retrieved the bun.

Sometimes on the journey to Youghal the train might be brought to a halt by cattle strolling on the line. While the train crew dealt with the situation the children would have their heads out the windows calling on them with such exhortations as: 'Come on, Charles Starrett, round them up!' The Durango Kid was a great favourite of youngsters. The story is told of a young man from the city who once got a job working in Glanmire Station. He was a hard-working conscientious ambitious fellow and in due course he was promoted. His new job meant travelling on the train every day and announcing the name of the various stations as the train arrived. There was a problem, however. He was unable to read and so the names of the stations written in large letters on the platforms availed him not. But he was nothing if not inventive and solved his dilemma by shouting aloud at each station: 'Is there anyone here for there?' The saying still lingers on in the memory of many a Corkonian. That railway worker knew how to use his head. He didn't get it for a hat.

Youghal has a fine safe strand that stretches for miles and having come from the narrow streets and lanes of the city we could only gaze in wonder at its expanse. The smell of the salt air wafted towards us immediately we alighted on the station platform. There we waited a short while to see the steam-engine being turned around and attached to the other end of the train in preparation for the journey back to Cork. Having overseen that operation being successfully concluded we then made our hurried way out through the gate of the station and down to the strand. At the gate the dillisk woman plied her trade and seemed to do so very successfully. Beside her women sold cockles, shouting out repeatedly: 'Get your fresh cockles here. Hold out yer buckets and I'll fill for ye at two-pence a go.' We loved the dillisk but balked at the cockles knowing that they had to be prized from their shells and eaten alive.

Once outside the gates of the station the older children would scamper off down to the strand ignoring the admonitions of their mothers who were stretched to keep up with them. Bringing up the rear were the reluctant fathers. In no time the children young and old were in the water splashing and dousing one another and filling the air with shrieks of delight. The women would take off their shoes and bathe their tired feed at the water's edge. The men remained fully clothed near the water, caps on heads, trousers rolled up just above the ankles, boots in hands as they sauntered along the wet sand barely allowing the spent waves to cover their toes. Even if the rain poured down most children ventured into the sea to frolic and prank knowing that they would not have such an opportunity again until the following summer.

The more timid amongst them and the women with younger children would retire to a covered shed to eat the food which they had brought with them. Boiling water could be bought at a shilling a kettleful from the owners of the timber bungalows that dotted the sea-front at Claycastle. Many of those bungalows had neither electricity nor running water, but to satisfy the demand they filled with water every utensil they could lay their hands on, enamel buckets, pots and dishes, and boiled them on primuses. But neither the prospect of food or a nice refreshing cup of tea could coax the disgruntled men into ceasing their moaning and groaning. It was a case of 'There's an awful bloody taste off that tea!' or 'There's sand in me sandwiches.' They hoped that such remarks would result in their deliverance from torture, and very often the ruse worked when a wife in desperation would say to her husband: 'Will you for God's sake go away up town to Clancy's pub with the rest of them and give us a bit of peace?'

The journey back to Cork in the evening took about an hour. Mothers with young children availed of the first train home to avoid the crush on later trains. There was far less noise in every carriage because the children were always tired out after a hectic day, except of course those who had suffered sunburn and were quite cranky. Mothers too were exhausted while the men who had escaped to the pub were high in colour around the gills, sweating profusely from a combination of heat and drink but much more mellow than earlier on. Children who had survived the day better than others would look out the window and gaze enthralled at the wonders of the countryside. It was on such a journey that many of them saw a rabbit for the first time, and as for myself the only time in my life that I saw a fox was on an excursion train to Youghal. As we approached Midleton Station he was pointed out to me scampering up the side of a field.

I have a very vivid recollection of one such annual trip to Youghal. It was on Sunday the first of September 1939. Lashing rain was accompanied by forked lightning which seemed intent on ripping the sky apart. My father was at the station to meet us on our return and carried a bundle of old coats in which to wrap us against the vile weather as we walked home. That same day a special edition of the *Echo* was printed informing the citizens that the Second World War had broken out. It seemed as if the elements were giving us a foretaste of the wanton destruction and bombings and slaughter that were soon to come. It was indeed a dismal day made even worse for us by the news that Kilkenny had beaten Cork by a solitary point in the All-Ireland Hurling Final.

A charitable group in Cork set up a very admirable scheme whereby poor children were enabled to go to Ringaskiddy and Ringabella on a week's holidays. The scheme was called the Fresh Air Fund and the children stayed with local families. Mam once availed of it to send a brother and sister of mine to Ringaskiddy. They stayed just one night there and the next day accompanied by other neighbours' children they left and walked all the way back home. It wasn't that they were dissatisfied with conditions. They were homebirds and missed the loving care of their families.

Many a time a group of us would go down to the bus office on the Grand Parade and take a bus to Blackrock for a picnic. Tickets cost two pence, a penny down and a penny back. Those picnics usually took place from St Patrick's Day onwards. Before leaving home we would gather up a few baats of bread and anything else that was available, a pinch of tea and an old gallon or tin. Having got out of the bus in Blackrock our first call always was to the local shop, not so much to spend our few half-pennies on sweets as to have an excuse to visit the parrot there which had a wide-ranging selection of curses and bad language. After enjoying his performance we would go up past the Castle and spend the day by the riverside. When the pangs of hunger began to make themselves felt we would gather up some sticks and rotted brambles, light a fire, boil our can of water and make tea and eat. If the weather wasn't too cold we might do a bit of paddling, but that usually entailed being covered up to our ankles in filthy mud as the area did not have a strand. However a visit to the nearby pump solved that problem and made us respectable again.

THE 'MONKS'

In the 1930s Cork Corporation embarked on a massive house-building programme in an effort to provide good alternative accommodation for people living in poor housing conditions in the city centre and in areas such as our own. To have any chance of getting a house in the estates which were being built one had to convince the Corporation officials that one's house deserved to be condemned. That meant a visit to the City Hall to state your case and if you did so convincingly an official was later sent to examine the house. Usually he gave the floors and the walls an especially thorough examination, and knowing this full well the occupants of the house had usually carried out some preparatory work to strengthen their argument! This entailed the removal of tarpaulin or whatever covering was on the floor, thus exposing the holes in the rotted timber. A few deft stabs with the heel of a shoe would result in some extra holes appearing in the timber while wallpaper that might have been hung years before to cover up dampness or even holes in the walls might be unceremoniously torn down to reveal the flaws. When the official came to inspect the house all the faults were pointed out to him and he noted them in his book and departed. If soon afterwards he failed to contact you to say your house was condemned you cursed him and said: 'The devil hoist him!' but if he condemned it you thought him the best and most understanding man in Cork.

In due course a little blue-coloured notice was attached to the outside of the front wall of our house informing all and sundry that the house had been condemned as being unfit for human habitation. We were naturally delighted, not just because we would not be obliged to pay further rent – landlords were not entitled to rent on condemned houses – but because the hopes of being given a new house were getting brighter by the day. Then those hopes were dashed when we learned that the new houses built in Greenmount on land which the Corporation had purchased from the Presentation Brothers had all been allotted, mostly to families from the Marsh in the centre of the city. We were not amongst the lucky ones. That was a severe blow because Mam was most anxious to continue to live within easy reach of Gran's house, and there was now a danger of our being moved a good distance away. But our luck was in – I like to think that somebody was praying for us – because not more than a few weeks later a letter arrived from the Corporation Housing Department stating that an almost new house in Greenmount, 18 Mount Sion Road, had become vacant due to a cancellation, and asking Mam to call to the City Hall to pick up the key. A new house, and in the 'Monks' too! That really was news to gladden the heart.

Mam immediately set off on foot for the City Hall. The official who gave her the key explained that the house had already been allotted to a lone woman who for years had been living in poor conditions in the Alms House in Peters Street. The Alms House was once the home of one of Cork's richest families. Later on alms used to be given to the poor there but with the passage of time it became a tenement with up to ten families and some lone people residing there. When this particular woman moved out to Mount Sion Road she found the new house too impersonal and extremely lonely. Admittedly she had spent her life in a big ramshackle house but there were families above her, below her and all around her and so she never knew loneliness. Living in a tenement you heard people passing up and down stairs throughout the day and much of the night too. You knew them by their step or the way they banged their door. It is small wonder then that many a person transferred from the inner city to what were then outlying areas experienced a real shock. Some idea of the disruption felt by such people can be gleaned from the fact that it took anything up to seven or eight new houses to accommodate all the occupants of one tenement, and the new houses allotted to them could be quite a distance apart from one another. This woman missed the company of her old friends and neighbours so much that she gave up her new house and went back where she belonged. Luckily she acquired another room for herself amongst her old friends in the Middle Parish. Restored to her former environment she was happy and so too were we.

Immediately Mam returned from the City Hall with the key she and all the family, inevitably accompanied by Gran, took off to see the new house which was now ours for three shillings and sixpence a week, sixpence cheaper than the house in Gunpowder Lane.

The sight of the new house thrilled us. There was a small garden in front and five steps led up to the front door. When Mam turned the key and we entered the first thing that struck us was the almost brand new wooden stairs. Then there was the large kitchen to the front with a gaslight suspended from the ceiling. On it were two chains, one of them to light the gas and the other to extinguish it. Oil lamps and paraffin would henceforth be a thing of the past for us even though we would still have to be content with candles in the bedrooms. The gas pipes jutting out of the wall indicated that with the acquisition of a gas cooker we could cook and roast and forget about the grid-iron. In the corner stood a silvery-coloured galvanised ash-bin. The sink, the draining-board and the larder where we could keep our food, represented a giant step-up in our standard of living.

At the back of the house there was a bathroom complete with toilet. The sheer size of the white enamelled bath frightened the lives out of us. We had never before seen anything like it, and so mesmerised were we that we straightaway jumped into it shoes and all. It was a far cry from the facilities, if one could call them that, in the house which we were about to vacate where at washtime on a Saturday the old tin tub with handles on it would be placed in front of a roaring fire and filled with hot water, and one by one we were deposited in it and restored to a state of cleanliness. I still have one of those tubs in memory of the days that were. From now on we could have a real honest-to-God bath, or could we? Gran surveyed it

87

for a moment, then turned around and said to Mam: 'Sure you couldn't put the poor children into that thing! They'd get their end. They'd die with the cold. But listen now all the same, couldn't you wash your blankets grand in it? You'd have plenty of scope.'

Gran's greatest fear was that anyone of us would catch a cold. If she ever saw us sitting on the stone flags outside her door she would immediately admonish us with: 'Get up out of that or you'll get a cold in your kidneys.' She watched us girls like a hawk and if our clothes were above our knees she remonstrated with us and that remonstration was not prompted by anything to do with morals but with the possibility of a cold in the kidneys. When nowadays I see a girl wearing a miniskirt I have visions of Gran running across the street to her, putting her hand on her knee to feel how cold it was and saying reprovingly: 'Your mother should be ashamed of herself to let you out like that. Don't you know what will happen? You'll get a cold in the kidneys.'

As well as being solicitous for our welfare Gran was also very anxious lest anything be misused. She saw no sense whatsoever in divesting oneself of all one's clothes and stepping into such a large contraption in a cold bathroom when one could perform the task with the comfort of the kitchen fire. Later on we were repeatedly reminded of her inventiveness because in fact we found that her suggestion about washing the blankets in the bath was an excellent one. Whenever the time came for them to be washed Mam would throw them into the bath and add a bucket of hot water. Blankets being made of wool would not take kindly to being washed by rubbing as one would do on a washing board, so having thrown a couple of penny packets of soap called Speed into the water one or two of us would take off our shoes and stockings, jump into the bath and trample on and squelch the blankets with our feet. The result was clean blankets and clean feet.

Having completed our inspection of the ground floor we dashed upstairs followed at a more leisurely pace by Mam and

Gran. There was one big bedroom to the front and Mam decided there and then that she would keep that for herself and the younger children while of the two small rooms at the back one was set aside for the older boys and the other for the older girls. While we were still doing the rounds of the house there was a knock on the front door. It was one our new neighbours who had moved in just two weeks earlier.

'I came to welcome ye to this place,' she said to Mam who duly thanked her for her kindness. 'Most of the new people around ye here,' she continued, 'are from the Marsh like myself. Many of us lived in the Alms House. I thought ye might feel this place strange so I'd like ye to know that ye're welcome.'

That was a most encouraging start.

Within a day or two we began to move our belongings from the old house into No 18. My brother Noel and myself set up a shuttle service transferring the smaller items in our trusty old pram and each time we made the journey we had to bring with us a three-legged milking stool to stand on so that we could reach the keyhole and let ourselves in. A man living further up the lane had a horse and car and he was engaged to remove the heavier furniture, but Mam was afraid to entrust our big statue of the Sacred Heart to him lest it be broken among all the other things in the car so it travelled in the safety of the pram. The night before we left Gunpowder Lane everything had been moved except the beds and a few other items that would be required overnight. At eight o'clock next morning we were roused out of our sleep by loud knocking on the door. The demolition men had come to pull the house down. Then we heard one of the workmen say: 'There's people still in bed in that house, sir.'

His boss, in between various curses and imprecations, muttered something and then announced in cultured but impatient tone: 'They should have been out of it by yesterday. Knock again and get them out fast.'

We all leapt out of bed in our shimmies and made a frantic

dash to dress ourselves and look respectable. Then Mam open-ed the door to the irate boss. 'Hurry on out,' he said. 'You're holding myself and my men up and that costs money, you know.'

He was clearly in no mood for bargaining or compromise so we got down immediately to the task of dismantling the beds and bringing the various components out to the horse and cart. It was then we noticed that our half-door was miss-ing. Obviously somebody had taken it more than likely for firewood. It certainly wasn't worth taking as a souvenir.

I must admit I shed no tears leaving the lane that morning. Though I had experienced many happy days there I was glad to see the old house being demolished because it had too many sorrowful memories for me. I thought of my father who had died while we lived there, and of the old woman who told us that it was an unlucky house. I wondered if in fact there was indeed a curse on it, but then again I knew that Mam would never entertain such a thought. She had complete faith in the grace and goodness of God. When trouble came her way she totally accepted it as the Lord's will, and never asked: 'What did I do wrong that God now allows this misfortune to befall me?' To protest in such a manner was to fly in the face of God, and that was something one should never do.

The memory of a terrifying experience which we had while living in the lane is still with me. I was sleeping at the end of my mother's bed one night when suddenly I was awakened by barking dogs. After a minute or two the barking stopped and three long wails one after the other rent the night air and seemed to swirl around the lane. It was more frightening than the air-raid siren in Tower Street that during the war used to ring out over the city every Saturday at noon to remind people of the procedures they should follow in the event of a bomb attack. The third wail was the most frightening of the three and made me double down under the bedclothes. Even then I clearly heard the screaming of a woman: 'Don't take her from me! Don't take her from me! Go away and leave her to me!'

I recognised the voice as that of a woman who lived a short distance up the lane on the other side. She seemed to be struggling to get out of her house and confront whoever had screamed. Soon afterwards I heard heavy footsteps passing our door. Terrified I called out to Mam. She had heard it all too, and tried to comfort me by saying: 'It's all right now. It's gone.' Next morning we learned that the footsteps were those of a guard who had come to the woman's house to break to her the sad news that a daughter of hers in St Finbarr's Hospital had just died unexpectedly. It seemed that practically everybody in the lane had heard the wailing and the women nervously whispered to one another: 'Did you hear the banshee last night?' Each of them was convinced that the wailing had occurred just outside her own door. For months afterwards I was terrified of going to bed and used to beg my mother to give me Aspro tablets to put me into a deep sleep but she refused.

Now that all our furniture had been moved to the new house we settled in quickly. For thirty shillings Mam bought a fine secondhand Black Prince gas stove and had it connected to the supply. That in itself was a major step forward. Then she set about painting the bedroom with a rose-coloured Anderson's water paint to make the walls look warmer. She decided to wallpaper the kitchen and I assisted her by mixing flour and water to make the paste. A few years later during the war I read in the *Echo* an article about the plight of the people of Stalingrad, now called Volgograd, who having been besieged for six months with no food getting through to them tried scraping the flour paste off the wallpaper in an effort to survive.

With the coming of spring Mam managed to spare a few shillings to buy a new spade, a fork and some seeds so that she could plant the garden to the rear of the house. We set some potatoes, peas and strawberry plants. We planted a hedge around the front garden and a rose bush in the middle and sowed marigold seeds in the bed under the window. 'All hands on deck!' was the cry but our inexperience in gardening was clearly emphasised when my brother Geoffrey put the fork through his shoe injuring his foot and had to have treatment in the South Infirmary. Our vegetables throve. Eventually we had fine potatoes but the peas never reached the pot because as they ripened we ate them out of the pods. We were not adverse to eating unripe strawberries either, but every time one of us ventured into the back garden Mam, suspicious of our intentions, would jump up from her machine and rush to the back window to warn us off the forbidden fruit. Her efforts were in vain, however, as one day some neighbouring children came through the dividing wire fence and relieved us of every single strawberry. It was a heartbreak.

News of my mother's ability with the sewing machine soon spread around the area and women began to call on her to do odd jobs for them. In the case of most of them money was in short supply so Mam rarely got the opportunity of working with new material. Her work consisted mainly of cutting up old skirts to make pants for boys, cutting down old coats and turning them inside out to make coats for the younger children and altering dresses and other garments for adults. The house was full of little bundles of clothes brought in for alterations. Very soon it became an open house with women coming and going all the time. Mam was a compassionate woman and a good listener. Knowing that she was one who could keep a secret many of the women confided in her and sought comfort from her in their trials and tribulations. They told her of their financial problems, how their children were getting on, their husbands and the trouble they were having with them. She was very different to Gran in that respect. Gran rarely allowed any of Granda's customers into her kitchen because she strongly disapproved of any talk that smacked of gossip or *dúirt sé dáirt sé* or, to use the Cork women's own favourite term, 'connishuring'.

Mam charged only a modest fee for her work as she appreciated the difficult circumstances in which many mothers found themselves. She rarely had any problems with them as the vast majority were good payers even though they might not have the money on the dot. My clearest recollection is of her pedalling furiously on her foot-machine trying to earn the extra few shillings which now and again might enable her to treat us with some little luxury for our tea. 'Take that pants up to the woman's house now,' she would sometimes say to me, 'and tell her that the price is one and sixpence. If she pays you, run down to Mary in the Dairy and get a shilling's worth of corned beef for the tea.'

When I arrived at the door the woman might say: 'Thank your Mam for me and tell her I'll hand the money in to her on Friday when I get the wages.'

My heart would sink then because I knew how partial Mam was to the corned beef. In such situations I would think of the day she met a friend of hers with her little daughter, an only child. They were on their way to town and Mam gave a penny to the girl who on being asked what she would do with the money answered: 'I'll buy a nice cake for myself.' A few hours later Mam happened to meet the mother and child on their way home from town.

'Well, Eileen,' she said to the little girl, 'did you buy the cake?'

'I didn't,' Eileen answered, 'I had to lend it to me mother to buy a duck-egg for her dinner.'

SERVANTS' ENTRANCE

Having finished with primary school I went into St Marie's of the Isle secondary school which, of course, would not have been possible had there been a fee to pay, but it is to the eternal credit of the nuns that they provided an excellent secondary education free of charge for those children whose parents could not afford to pay. I was in Second Year when I reached my fourteenth birthday, the day to which we children all looked forward so eagerly, because on that day we could say goodbye to school and move out into the great big world. In spite of the nuns' pleading with us to continue at school and assurances that we would do well there we left. We wanted to be independent. A great new life was beckoning outside and we wished to be part of it. We envied our older sisters as we watched them go out to pictures and dances, smoke cigarettes and wear lipstick. We were beginning to have an interest in boys too. Radios were becoming plentiful. They provided the latest in music and song and so we wanted one of our own. Underlying all that too was the knowledge that financially things weren't good at home and if we got work we could help ease our parents' burden, and maybe buy a radio on the hire purchase system, known as the Kathleen Mavourneen: 'it may be for years and it may be forever.'

Weeks before I left school I started to scan the Situations Vacant column in the *Echo* and came across an advertisement which read: 'Help wanted in house in Douglas area, twelve shillings and sixpence a week plus a shilling bus fare'. That was rather above the going rate for domestic work so I replied to the advertisement and within a few days received a letter requesting me to go to the house in question for an interview. My prospective employer gave me very clear directions as to where she lived and so I had no problem in locating the house. I crunched my way up the gravelled drive to this big house with its extensive garden full of shrubs and flowers. I approached the front door, lifted the knocker and let it drop down gently. Within seconds the door opened and the lady of the house appeared walking with the aid of a stick. She had a face on her like thunder which left me with a definite sense of foreboding.

'You're not from a family who have any experience of service,' she almost hissed. 'If you were you would have been told never to come to the front door, so in future go around the back and come in the servants' entrance.'

I had learned my first lesson. The back door was for mere servants and tradesmen. That was my first encounter with something I had never experienced in the lanes. It is known as class distinction. She brought me into the kitchen and proceeded to question me on my background and on other matters which she deemed relevant. She wasn't at all impressed to learn that none of my family had any experience of domestic service but after some further interrogation she reluctantly agreed to give me a six months' trial. It seemed as though she felt I was the best of a bad lot of applicants, if indeed there were any others, because a scarcity of young domestic girls existed at that particular time. The papers carried advertisements every day offering young girls work in houses in England at a far higher wage than applied here in Ireland. Their fares across were paid as well as whatever expense was involved in procuring travel documents. All a girl had to do was to call to the agency on the Grand Parade and everything, including her fare, was taken care of. She could then sail on the *Innisfallen* to a new life across the Irish Sea. I was never attracted by the prospect of living in England and so was happy to stay in Cork if any reasonable job materialised.

The morning I began work in Douglas I walked over to the top of High Street, carrying under my arm a new pair of house-shoes which my employer had told me would be necessary. At High Street I boarded the Douglas bus and a penny ticket brought me as far as the house in ample time for my half-past nine start. The first task assigned to me was the polishing of the family's shoes. Then I was directed to the morning-room and told to clear the breakfast ware from the table. Any crumbs that had fallen on the table I had to brush into a silver salver with a small white brush and bring them to the kitchen where they were put aside to be used at a later stage as a thickening for soup. A small amount of water was mixed with the few drops of milk remaining in the jug and this mixture then set aside as a base for the soup at dinner-time. That done I was ordered to brush the morning-room with a short-handled brush and scoop the dust into a dust-pan. The next task was to put a dustcloth on a mop and shine up the linoleum. Subsequently I was informed that I would have to polish the linoleum once a week. It was hard work but that was something of which I was never afraid. Indeed I took a pride in doing it to the best of my ability. The other rooms had to be dusted and polished regularly also.

Occasionally the old woman would stand over me as I polished her massive silver salvers and candlesticks and the many valuable trophies around the house. She gave me a special powder with which to polish the silver items and a special short-haired brush to clean that powder from the ornamental crevices. Brushing the many luxurious carpets was to prove a major chore made all the more tiring because, due to the inadequate equipment available, I had to perform the work on my hand and knees. Once a week I scrubbed the limestone steps leading up to the front door, those selfsame steps which I was deemed to have defiled on the morning of my interview. I clearly recall the first time I scrubbed them. It was a beautiful soft May morning. The gardener had just mown the spacious lawn when a light shower of rain fell, and then my nostrils were assailed by the gorgeous aroma of freshly-cut grass and flowers. It was something I had never previously experienced and will not forget to my dying day.

Having washed the breakfast ware each morning I then had to clean and prepare the vegetables for dinner. This I did under the cold tap in the kitchen, and it was my only involvement in the preparation of the midday meal which was invariably cooked by the daughter of the house. She was no spring chicken, yet she spent practically all her time playing tennis. She never spoke to me except for the odd occasion when she wished to give me directions or ask me some question about work. Neither did the other two family members, father and son, over-exert themselves in making conversation with me, but at least it could be said in their favour that they were rarely in the house during my six-day week because they were engaged in business in town and never came home during the day. Mother and daughter ate their dinner in the morning-room, but before I ate mine, in the kitchen needless to say, I was required to ring a bell at the back door to summon the gardener. On his arrival I handed him his dinner on a tray whereupon he retired to eat it in the tool-shed.

In fairness, however, I must admit that the standard of the food was very high. There for the first time in my life I had the pleasure of having a thick mutton chop all to myself. The vegetables were fresh and direct from the back garden and included kale which I had never previously tasted. I detested however the day that salad was on the menu. Salad was never on the table of any house in Gunpowder Lane and Gran's oft-stated opinion of it was that lettuce was fit only for rabbits and there was no bond whatever in it as there was in beef-tea, meat and eggs. If there was bond in the food which you got as a child it stood to you for the rest of your life. The hard-boiled eggs I would eat but the beetroot, lettuce and salad dressing I scraped off the plate into a bag which in turn I slipped into my coat-pocket and dumped on the way home. Dessert was always the same, an apple, but not even the crinkly skin like that of a prune prevented me from enjoying it. The apples came from the house orchard, but I never in fact set foot in that same orchard nor indeed in the vegetable garden either, because I had been warned early on that both places were strictly out of bounds for me though I was never told why.

When it came to the weekly wash the family was not dependent on a sawdust fire to heat the water as many a family known to me was. Their financial independence meant that they were able to purchase a large supply of coal before the outbreak of war, and because they used it sparingly the coalshed was still quite full. On wash-morning the gardener started up the boiler and when the water was heated I set about the washing, usually supervised by the hawk-eyed old lady. Her primary concern seemed to be that I might damage the various woollen garments by treating them too vigorously.

'Just squeeze them gently,' she would admonish me as I removed from the water her menfolk's long johns which bore labels that proclaimed them to have been made of pure new wool. 'Put them through the mangle from the neck,' she would direct me, 'or you'll knock them all out of shape.'

Never once did I have to wash the clothes with wartime soap because she had a stock of pre-war Ryan's Soap Flakes that would have seen her through for many a year to come.

I suffered agony every afternoon I worked in that house. The old lady mapped out my duties and the order in which I was to fulfil them while she retired for her siesta. My first duty was to boil two kettles of water with which to wash the dinnerware before the gas supply, which was subject to rationing, was cut off. While the water was being boiled I had to polish the floor of the large hall which often meant that by the time I had completed that chore the water had almost gone cold. Yet I was expected to wash the greasy ware with it. Refreshed by her siesta the old lady would enter the kitchen to check my work. Taking up the plates she would run her finger along them and then follow with the inevitable comment: 'Look at those plates. You don't mean to tell me that they're washed properly. There's still grease on them.'

I would have loved to have given her the answer she deserved but I felt that discretion was the better part of valour. My hand was in the dog's mouth and I was ever conscious of the fact that Mam needed every penny I could earn. So I would hang my head and keep a grip on my tongue. The old jade scourged and scalded me, yet to this day I can honestly say that I bear her no hatred because it may well be that her cantankerousness was due to her ill-health and infirmity. There was one thing, however, which I feel could not be excused on the grounds of her ill-health. The very first morning I went to work for her I noticed an Irish penny on the kitchen dresser. I immediately sensed that it was placed there to test my honesty but I am glad to say that that penny with its hen and clutch of chickens still occupied the same place on the dresser the day I left as it did the day I started there.

Even though the family lived in luxury they rarely entertained any friends, and if ever a visitor came to the front door uninvited I was to inform them politely: 'My mistress is not at home to visitors at present.' Admittedly those were the war years and food was rather scarce but the family was not too badly hit by shortages and rationing because they had stockpiled lots of food of various kinds before the commencement of the war and their larder was still rather full. It was, of course, always kept locked and I knew scarcely anything about its contents.

As time went on the old lady's constant carping began to take its toll of me and some time after I had completed my six months' trial, I thought it time to seek pastures new, even though she informed me of her intention to retain my services. I had recourse once again to the *Echo*, and before very long I saw an advertisement for young girls to train as shirtmakers in Dwyer's shirt-factory in Hanover Street. I applied and a few days after the interview I received a letter from the firm requesting me to start work at eight-thirty on the following Monday morning. I dared not tell the old lady of my impending departure as she would certainly have made my life a hell during my remaining few days. Neither did I dare return for my houseshoes which I forgot to take home with me, so Mam asked one of my sisters to retrieve them. The old lady left my sister in no doubt as to what she thought of me and my failure to notify her of my intention to leave

The Dwyer family are remembered with gratitude even today for the employment which they provided for thousands of Cork people in their various factories, particularly in the Sunbeam Wolsey factory on the Commons Road where they had a thriving knitwear and nylon stocking manufacturing business. Most of their factories were situated in the centre of the city, and from about eight o'clock every morning in every lane and street one could hear the sound of high heels click-clacking along the footpaths as hundreds of women made their way to work in the Lee Hosiery factory in the North Main Street and the shirt-factory where I myself was about to take up employment. The two boot factories owned by Dwyers, the Lee Boot in Washington Street and the Hanover in Hanover Street, provided hundreds of men and women with employ-ment. From the hills of the Northside to the gentler slopes of the Southside employees wended their way to work on foot and returned home each evening also on foot. Not for them the luxury of buses or cars. Shanks' mare was their only mode of travel and it didn't cost them a thought.

On Monday morning I arrived at the factory bright and early and eager to start work, and there for the first time I ex-perienced something I had so often heard about but never ex-perienced. It was known as 'clocking-in'. This operation was strictly enforced by a forelady whose job it was to see that the door was closed exactly at the eight-thirty starting-up time. She would stand on the landing inside the door and as the dead-line approached she would scream down at us as we hurried in: 'Shut that door! Do you hear me? Shut that door!' But we always tried to gain that precious moment or two which would enable the stragglers behind us to get in. The forelady on the stairs would dash down and slam the door in their faces. Being thus locked out meant that one could not clock in again until two in the afternoon, thereby losing a half-day's wages. In that event the locked-out girls on a fine day spent the morning in Fitzgerald's Park, and on bad days they killed the time meand-ering around the shops in the city centre. They were afraid to go home and let their parents know what had happened, so they preferred to endure the loss of earnings rather than suffer parental reproof.

The fact that my mother had years earlier taught me how to work a foot-machine was largely responsible for my getting the job in Dwyer's and provided me with a great head-start. I was detailed to work on a machine in the area where boys' shirts were manufactured. Several other young girls were also employed there while the older women were engaged in making men's shirts. The cutter would cut out enough pieces of material for a dozen shirts and it was our task to collect the pieces of material, sew them together and make the shirts. Our rate of pay was three shillings and sixpence a dozen. The work was light and clean and presented no problems, and I found the company and the camaraderie of the girls a wonderful change from the lonely circumstances under which I worked in Douglas.

At that time boys and girls who had left school at the age of fourteen were obliged to attend for a further two years a one day a week course run by the City of Cork Vocational Education Committee in their Parnell Square premises. I avoided going while I was in Douglas but there was an agreement whereby those in employment were released by their employers to attend the course so I had to go. As far as I was concerned I benefited little from it as most of the curriculum had already been covered during my St Marie's of the Isle schooldays. Cookery formed part of the VEC course but when I told Mam what the teacher there considered to be a dinner fit for a man – a mound of mashed potatoes and four sausages jutting like horns out of them – her reply was: 'The Lord save us, that's no dinner for a man. Don't take any notice of her, girl.' And to be honest I didn't.

We young girls were looked upon with disdain by some of the older women who considered us scatterbrained. We weren't unduly worried, however, and continued on our merry way talking about interesting and important subjects such as films, dances, boys and girls and dates. There I learned to smoke, and of course smoking was to us the definitive badge of adulthood although few of us would risk smoking at home in the presence of our parents. Having clubbed in for a halfpenny packet of five Woodbines five of us would on our way home from work adjourn to a tenement house in Millard Street where the tenants had no objection to our sitting on the stairs puffing a Woodbine each. The woman on the ground floor frequently passed us on her way out to the back-yard to throw out the dirty water and fill her kettle with clean water from the outside tap, but she never expressed any displeasure at our presence. Nowadays whenever I pass the site of that old tenement I offer up a silent prayer for the wonderful people who once inhabited it.

A Half-Ounce of Tea

The outbreak of the Second World War in September 1939 had a traumatic effect on the people of Cork, particularly the poor whose circumstances up to then were difficult and who now feared that the coming hostilities and inevitable rationing would render matters far worse. We children could sense our parents' anxieties but luckily for us most of their worries passed over our heads. We were far too young to have any idea as to what could happen if Ireland were invaded and so we carried on with our little lives in blissful ignorance.

Shortly after the war began rationing of various commodities was introduced, but the scarcity of essential foodstuffs hit hardest of all. Every householder in the country was obliged to register with a shopkeeper and give the number of people in the house so that each family got their due ration of tea, sugar and butter, as well as soap and other such commodities. Mam registered with Hynes' shop at the corner of Gilabbey Street and Bishop Street, where she had a weekly payment book, while Gran who paid cash for everything she bought registered with the Home and Colonial Stores in Princes Street. Each person was entitled to a weekly ration of three-quarters of an ounce of tea and three-quarters of a pound of sugar. Prior to the start of the war my mother, sensing that tea would surely be rationed, had been stocking some up according as her finances would allow, and that tea done up in red packets was put aside in a cupboard. Unfortunately she later ran short of money and had to dip into her tea reserves with the result that by the time the war began we had none left. Gran's biggest problem was the tea because with four adults in the house her total weekly ration amounted to a miserable three ounces. Some know-all advised her that by putting a spoon of bread soda into every pot of tea she made she would be able to draw more out of the leaves. She followed this advice all during the war period, and even took to drying the used tea-leaves and using them a second time. I cannot say how far the bread soda stretched the tea, if at all, but I would hazard a guess that it did nothing for Gran's stomach! Even the availability of coffee and Irel now and again availed us not at all because no one would ever dream of drinking either. My first experience of coffee was when in later years a young man invited me into a restaurant for a snack. Pretending to be grand I accepted his invitation to have a cup of coffee – after all only the rich drank the stuff – but to me that evening it tasted as foul as anything that ever passed my lips. It served me right for trying to show off.

The rationing of sugar was a great source of frustration for Mam because on no account would any of her offspring drink tea without sugar. She used to get our ration on Friday and come Monday it would have been used up. She would then ask one of us to run down to Mrs Hynes to inquire if she could give us a half-pound out of the following week's ration. That poor lady must have been driven to distraction trying to keep our account in order. In an effort to please our palates Mam sometimes put crushed barley-sugar sweets into our tea but in fact the sweetened Killarney Condensed Milk was more to our liking. When that in turn became unavailable she resorted to the tinned Limerick Half-cream. With her scissors she would punch a hole in the tin and put two level teaspoonfuls into each cup for us. To this very day I loathe milky tea but whether my experiences in those days are in any way responsible for that I cannot say. We had more than enough butter for our requirements because children were allowed an extra ration, so Mam used to give one pound of it, two shillings' worth, to another woman whose two working sons required it for their lunches, and in return she got a two-pound pot of jam, one shilling and nine pence worth, with a few boxes of matches added in to make up the price differential. Jam also was very scarce but as one of that woman's boys worked in Musgrave's he was in a position to get some every week. The jampots were made of an inferior dark green glass which did nothing to

104

enhance the appearance of the jam, particularly the apricot variety. All jams contained a lot of apple to help make the various fruits go farther but the jams were accordingly less palatable. I was aware, however, that Gran always had a pot of pure strawberry jam in her cupboard downstairs – the Home and Colonial Stores where she shopped succeeded from time to time in getting a small supply – and now and again, while she enjoyed her afternoon nap, I would steal down the two flights of stairs, open the cupboard silently, stick my two fingers in the pot, and extract a few strawberries. They always tasted divine.

The rationing of the various commodities prompted some unknown bard to compose a parody on the British army song 'Bless 'em all' that became very well-known throughout the country and a few snippets of which I still remember:

> Bless 'em all, bless 'em all,
> The long and the short and the tall;
> Bless de Valera and Seán McEntee
> Who gave us brown bread and the half ounce of tea.
> Sure they rationed the sugar and all
> That should not be rationed at all.
> They're bringing starvation to our little nation,
> So cheer up, me lads, one and all.
>
> Hitler's coming to Ireland next week
> To visit the Blarney Stone.
> There he'll dig a trench forty feet deep
> So that the angels can tickle his feet.
> And then Mussolini comes next
> With medals all over his chest.
> The brown bread is killing, the half-ounce is filling,
> So cheer up, me lads, one and all.

White bread was unavailable in the shops and the only bread on sale was of an unappetising coarse quality. We hated it. White flour too was non-existent, and the only flour available contained a generous amount of bran that had little appeal for us. If a woman wished to make a rich cake at Christmas time

105

or for a wedding perhaps, she would sieve the flour. Of course there wasn't a sieve in the whole of our street. That was an appliance that didn't form part of any kitchen equipment in our area and the only time I ever saw one was in the cookery class in school. So necessity being the mother of invention somebody found out that a lady's nylon stocking could solve the problem. You put the flour into the stocking which you then shook vigorously. The flour came out through the nylon and the bran remained inside. Luckily for the women of Cork nylon stockings were rather plentiful because the Sunbeam Knitwear factory in Blackpool had been making them since shortly before the outbreak of war. The women of England were not so lucky and it was rumoured that many a wily Cork person took the boat to England and made good money there by smuggling those stockings to sell on the black market.

Cigarettes became extremely scarce and one needed to keep on exceptionally good terms with the local shopkeepers to be assured of even an intermittent supply. Cork smokers loved Woodbines, a cheap but strong brand costing just two pence for an open-ended packet of five. Kerry Blues and Players' Weights, known usually as coffin nails, were the cheapest varieties of all and resorted to only when no Woodbines were available. It was a case of 'when all fruit fails welcome haws'. Butts, even those found on the streets, were collected, and five of them rolled together made one cigarette. Women did not smoke but their menfolk depended on them to keep them supplied. Cigarettes were never on display on shop shelves. They were always hidden under the counter, and women were often heard to say: 'Them shopkeepers will end up with humps on their backs from all the bending down.' If a woman entered a shop and observed the shopkeeper reaching under the counter for cigarettes for a favoured customer she would take the ball on the hop by saying: 'As you're stooping there, Mr O', I'll have a packet too.'

I am reminded of a story I once heard from a countryman who as a young boy worked on a big demesne. His aristocratic employer sent him into the nearby town for a carton of cigarettes. Having been handed the carton by the shopkeeper the boy bought a packet of five Woodbines for himself, the maximum he could afford. On his return to the domain he handed the carton to his employer and then proceeded to light a Woodbine for himself. In the process the five Woodbines fell out of the packet into a bucket of lime and water which he had been using to whitewash an outhouse. His employer, with the carton under his arm, said cynically as he walked away: 'It's a great thing to have money!' There and then the young boy vowed he would never again depend on the likes of him for a living, so he saved every penny he earned and in due course bought his own farm.

From the outset of the war coal became exceedingly scarce so we had to resort to other types of fuel to do the cooking and keep the fires going. Turf was the main substitute and I got my first glimpse of it when a lorryload was brought into Ninety Eight Street and sold at a shilling a bag. The subsequent smell of burning turf emanating from the chimneys was completely new to us but we found it pleasant. Much of the turf coming into the city was diabolical, indeed it was so wet that one could squeeze the water out of it. It was widely believed that those supplying it threw water on it to make it heavier. However we realised later that bad weather during the turf-cutting season was mainly responsible. Turf was sold only through certain depots, the nearest of which was in Barrack Street. If the turf there was wet Mam would walk to the depot in Douglas Street and from there to another one across the river in the Marsh to see which offered the driest. Some families lucky enough to have a range would, when the fire was lighting, place wet sods on top to dry. On our return from school in the afternoon we used to take the pram or the boxcar to the chosen depot, load up the turf and push it all the way home.

A boxcar was an invaluable asset to any household. Its construction was simplicity itself. You procured a timber box three feet by two perhaps, attached to its bottom a pair of old ball-bearing pram-wheels, and nailed two timber shafts on to it, one at either side. The irritating sound of unlubricated box-car-wheels was one of the commonest sounds on the streets of Cork in those days. Often on Saturday mornings my brother Noel and myself were sent down to the Gasworks for slack. Many is the time the snow and ice were thick on the ground as we pushed our boxcar down past St Fin Barre's Cathedral, on to French's Quay, O'Sullivan's Quay and George's Quay, along South Terrace, across Anglesea Street and up the hill to Hibernian Buildings, more commonly known as Jewtown, where the Gas Company had their depot. There we would stand in a line of people and boxcars – the word 'queue' had not as yet become part of our vocabulary – waiting for our load of slack. When we got home Mam with her bare hands mixed the slack with water and formed the mixture into egg-shaped lumps which she always referred to as duck eggs.

The much-maligned sawdust often came to our aid when fuel was scarce. We bought it by the bag from Haughton's in South Terrace or else from Hurley's Mills in nearby Bishop Street who also sold the bark of native trees. On Monday mornings the sawdust fire was prepared to do the weekly wash in Gran's backyard. An oil drum with a piece hacked out of the bottom to create a draught was placed on two bricks. A sweeping-brush was placed upright in the centre of the drum so that it protruded out through the hole in the bottom. Then the sawdust was packed tightly up to the top of the drum and finally the brush was withdrawn upwards and a lighted piece of newspaper placed in the hole underneath to ignite the sawdust. The ensuing smokeless blazeless fire provided three or four hours' red heat. A piece of iron placed across the top of the drum held the galvanised buckets which contained water and washing soda, and in quite a short time the water was boiled and the washing soda dissolved. Then the water was poured into the bath-tub and the timber washing-board was brought out.

One of my oldest memories is that of seeing Mam or Gran with sleeves rolled up rubbing the clothes up and down the ridges of the board. Occasionally they used a black soap with the name Sambo stamped on it. After the wash had been completed a tub was placed under the outside tap to rinse the clothes. When white bedlinen and handkerchiefs were to be washed a Reckitt's blue-ball was placed in the water turning it a deep blue colour. That helped to whiten the clothes and prevent yellowing. On wet days the washing was done in Gran's rather primitive washhouse which was simply an extension to the outdoor toilet, the 'house of parliament'. There were kept the timber tubs, hanging from large iron brads hammered into the wall, and also the mangle and washing board.

Some local boys succeeded in locating an alternative though rather unsatisfactory source of fuel along the West Cork Railway line. This consisted of clinkers thrown out of the steam-engine by the fireman. These they packed into bags to carry home and later broke them into small pieces to be used at the back of the fire. Everything in the house that could be burned was burned, including old chairs, boots, lino and gramophone records. I even saw Mam pulling two paintings of Killarney off the wall in an effort to set some wet turf alight. 'I never liked them anyway,' she said, as she tore them up. 'They were too dark and dreary for my liking.'

Paraffin oil was another commodity the scarcity of which affected us greatly. As we did not have electricity in our house we depended on paraffin to provide light. Mam would regularly place us children at strategic lookout points in the area in the hope that we might see an oil-lorry passing the way, and if we did we dashed home, grabbed the money and the oil-can and joined dozens of other children racing through the streets after the disappearing lorry. Sometimes it might stop at Irwin's on Bandon Road, the nearest shop to us that sold oil. Other times it might not and then we had to chase it down to Healy's at the corner of Step Lane and Barrack Street. Wherever it stopped we had to stand in a line with all the other children awaiting our turn for the precious liquid.

Petrol was severely rationed and apart from industrial

firms the only people who could get any were doctors, priests and members of a few other categories involved in providing essential services. The amount which even they got was meagre. Many vans and lorries were converted to run on gas and soon became a familiar sight with their gas-tanks on top of the cab like large yellow balloons. We ourselves had one consolation. At least the scarcity of petrol did not render our boxcars immobile! The Great Southern Railway Company, removal firms, bakeries, funeral undertakers and various other business concerns depended almost entirely on the horse for transport with the result that that noble animal played a vital role in the life of the city.

There must be few cities anywhere in the world with a terrain so unkind to draught-horses as Cork which resembles a soup-bowl with steep hills on every side. But most drivers were kind and considerate to their horses and if they thought it necessary they would, on coming to a hill, jump out of the cart, take the horse by the bridle and enlist any man who might be passing to go round to the back and push with all his might until the horse reached the summit and was given a breather. Some carts or drays were drawn by a pair of horses, and children gazed in admiration as the driver took his position between the horses and coaxed and cajoled them up the hill. As the horses strained under the weight of the load the veins in their necks stood out like ropes. Most of them were so quiet and so accustomed to the city streets that they could practically find their own way around, but now and again one might take fright and bolt. That was when the excitement began, but even the city men knew what to do in such a situation and they would run out on to the middle of the street waving their arms and attempting to stop the frightened animal. Horses often became very attached to their masters and the story is told of one man who drove a horse for his employer. He worked hard but his wage was small and so he asked for a rise. His employer turned down what was to him an audacious request so the man left his job. A new man was hired in his place but the horse refused to budge an inch for him, with the result that the employer had to eat humble pie and re-employ the first man at the wage he had requested.

It was a grand sight to stand in Washington Street after business hours of a summer's evening and watch three, four or maybe five colossal shire or draught-horses with their iron shoes knocking sparks out of the street surface as they trotted past on their way to pasture and a well-earned over-night rest in the Lee Fields. A lone young lad, perched like a pimple high up on the back of one of them, would have a reins attached to each animal all the while talking and urging them on with 'Come on, me beauties!' or 'Up me hairy lads!'

Many bakeries had their stables quite close to people's homes. Lannin's Bakery had stables just a few doors down from Granda's shop, Simcox's Bakery had theirs in Kyrl Street, and O'Shea's Bakery stables were in a laneway off the South Main Street. The railway horses were stabled in a quiet area just above the station.

As bus and train excursions to the seaside ceased completely owing to the fuel shortage people took to the road on their trusted bicycles. Crosshaven became the most popular resort being only about fifteen miles away. Another regular sight on the roads on fine Sundays were the wagonettes each drawn by a pair of horses. How I envied boys and girls in their teens or slightly older as they packed into the wagonettes seated facing one another and set off for 'Crosser', their faces aglow with happiness and a gadget player in their midst to play the latest hits along the way! All joined in the singing. Many of them, naturally enough, were experiencing love's young dream, perhaps for the first time, but there were also mature couples with them just to make sure that they didn't get up to too many shenanigans. Going up Carr's Hill the more energetic passengers got out of the wagonette and walked behind so as to ease the burden on the horses.

Donkeys, mules and jennets also contributed their share to transport, admittedly at a more leisurely pace, but they were consigned to very second-class accommodation in cowlucks and ruins. I remember one man who kept his donkey in the yard at the back of his house, and on its way to or from the yard the donkey had to pass through the kitchen and hallway. The man himself was as odd as two left feet. One day I watched him straining every muscle in his body as he helped the donkey pull a load up Bishop Street past St Fin Barre's Cathedral. Having reached the top he leaned his back against the wall to regain his breath. Suddenly the donkey started to heehaw. His owner became irate and roared out: 'You rotten hoor, you're laughing at me!' Were it not for the intervention of a few onlookers he would have brought the poor animal down the hill again and made him pull the load up a second time, unaided perhaps.

A great civic spirit made itself evident among the people after the war began. Many young men joined the army which was much bigger than at any time previous. Older men, some of whom had experience with guns in the War of Independence, joined the Local Defence Force, familiarly known as the LDF. This force, as the name implies, was a part-time body established to assist the regular army by providing extra security throughout the country. Joining the LDF appealed to many people for a reason that had nothing at all to do with patriotism. Each member on joining was given a big green heavy overcoat but instead of using it for the purpose for which it was obviously intended most people used it as an extra blanket on the bed on cold winter nights. It therefore became commonly known as the 'green eiderdown'. Dad joined the LDF while a few of my cousins joined another group called the ARP, or Air Raid Precaution. The latter group strutted proudly around with tin helmets on their heads and a brown first-aid box slung over their shoulders.

At the time there were great fears that Ireland would be drawn into the war by one side or the other and so air-raid shelters were hastily erected in the city, as indeed they were in other cities also. These were long low ugly mass-concrete buildings. The nearest one to us was in Dean Street. Others were erected in French's Quay, the Marsh and the Grand Parade. The slatted timber doors of these shelters were all painted green, and peeping through the slats all one could see within was emptiness and gloom. Thank God at no time during the war had the people of Cork to avail of the protection offered by such shelters, which was just as well because in the event of an aerial attack I imagine the shelters would have availed them very little. If a stampede took place where would they all find room? Gas-masks were supplied to all the citizens and came in three sizes, large, medium and small, and I recall my parents on a dark drizzly night having to march us all down to a room at the back of the courthouse to be fitted with them. It was a frightening experience for any child to be fitted with that same contraption.

Few homes had a radio in those days. My uncle Sam who lived downstairs with Granda did have a crystal set with earphones draped across the gas bracket but we were warned of the dire consequences that would result if we even as much as touched it. For any home which did not have a radio the *Echo* was the main source of news concerning the progress of the war and was therefore in great demand. It fell to me every evening to go down to Johnny Chisholm's shop at the corner of Warren's Lane for the *Echo*. With my penny clutched firmly in my hand I would sit on the kerb outside waiting for Johnny to appear round the corner of the street with the big bundle of papers tied on the handlebars of his bicycle. Having got my copy I would then dash back home where Granda anxiously awaited its arrival. He would then suspend all work. He would first place a map of the world on the counter and carefully study the events of the war as described on the paper. Later on men on their way home from work would call into the shop more hungry for war news than for their dinner. Tactics were discussed, opinions given and judgements made so seriously that one could be forgiven for thinking that the gathering was a high-powered meeting of military leaders.

People became increasingly anxious as the atrocities of the war unfolded in print before their eyes. Fears were particularly high after the Taoiseach Eamon de Valera refused Churchill's request that some Irish ports, including Cobh, be handed over for use by the allies. Then there was the episode involving the unarmed *SS Kerlogue,* the crew of which *en route* from Portugal to Ireland plucked well over a hundred German sailors from the sea after their boat had been torpedoed. On learning this the British naval authorities were enraged and threatened the *Kerlogue* crew with dire consequences unless they handed over the Germans but the crew resolutely refused to do so and brought them back to Ireland. When it was learned that the *Kerlogue* had docked at Cobh scores of Cork people cycled there in the hope of getting a glimpse of the Germans before they were transferred to the Curragh internment camp where they spent the remainder of the war years. The Irish people owe a great debt of gratitude to the brave crews of such ships as the *Kerlogue* who braved mine-infested seas and attacks from sea and air in their efforts to bring in essential goods. Many of them unfortunately went to an untimely watery grave.

As the war advanced the tea ration was reduced to a half-ounce a week per person while sugar was reduced to a half-pound. To relieve the food situation in the city the government extended an existing scheme whereby plots of ground were parcelled out free of charge to families to grow their own vegetables and potatoes. The Northside people were allotted plots near the Blarney Road while the Southsiders including ourselves were given theirs near Ducks' Pond at the western end of College Road. My uncle was allotted a plot and on paying a nominal charge he was given a shovel, a fork and a bag of seed potatoes. My grandfather cut the potatoes into skillauns while sitting on a chair with two buckets, one on either side of his feet. One bucket contained lime and as he cut the potatoes he dipped each skillaun into the lime and then threw it into the other bucket. The use of lime on skillauns was then widespread but it is now considered to be harmful to the tubers.

The plots were generally speaking a great success and many a city-born man who had never before stuck a fork in the ground managed to grow potatoes, cabbage and onions for his family. This novel work gave rise to many a wisecrack such as 'Did you hear that German planes invaded the plots?'

'My God no. Why did they do that?'

'They were looking for British Queens!'

Those plots were side by side in open fields, but to the eternal credit of the people not a potato or a vegetable of any kind was ever stolen.

England's food scarcity during the war was in many ways Ireland's opportunity. It was said locally that the cats here had more meat available to them than the people of England. That was probably a reference to Mary the Cats who lived not far from us in Canty's Field. Every day of her life she passed down our street, a wicker basket hanging from her arm, on her way to the butcher's shop where she collected offal and animal lights to feed the cats of the neighbourhood. She looked upon them as her family.

England's shortage of meat meant that she was happy to buy it from us in any shape or form. This situation offered an opening even to enterprising schoolboys. They would mitch from school – 'going on the lang' as it was known – and go down to the quays where hundreds of plump pigeons gathered in search of food and grain. The pigeons had become accustomed to the hustle and bustle there and were quite tame. This, of course, made them rather easy prey for the boys who caught them with improvised lassos and found a ready market for them from the exporters. One exporter dirtied his bib when he was caught sending out pigeons as small chickens!

Ferreting rabbits in those pre-mxyomatosis times provided a welcome source of revenue to those enterprising men who every day cycled out to the fields around Bishopstown, each of them with a ferret or maybe two in a bag, a few small nets and a terrier perched precariously on the bike with its backside on the crossbar and front legs on the handlebar. Rabbit burrows ran through fences like an underground railway system with each burrow having more than one exit. The men would cover with nets all the exits save one into which they would put the ferret complete with a bell around his neck. By putting their ears close to the various exits the men could, with the aid of the bell, tell the ferret's whereabouts inside. Then the excitement began. The well-trained ferret did not kill but hunted the rabbits to the exits where the men awaited them. Even if a few rabbits did succeed in slipping through the nets eager terriers lay in wait for them outside so that escape was almost out of the question. Come evening the hunters returned triumphantly with the rabbits hanging by their hind legs from the handlebars. Rabbits fetched good money, a shilling and sixpence a head and sometimes more, from Lane's the exporters in nearby Cat Lane.

During the second half of the war England experienced an extreme shortage of fruit for jam-making. That provided the opportunity for us children, particularly the girls, to make a few 'lops', pennies to people unlucky enough not to be well-versed in the Cork lingo. In late summer and early autumn with our galvanised buckets dangling from our hands we would set forth to pick blackberries in Lehenagh Wood or Cáit Shea's Boreen now known as Rossa Avenue, or along the West Cork Railway line towards the Viaduct. I usually picked with my brother Noel because he was a fast picker and did not eat very many but kept them for sale. I can remember to this day that each bucket held sixteen pounds which at four pence a pound earned us two shillings and eight pence each. When the buckets were full we covered the contents with ferns to take them home and before selling them we weren't averse now and again to throwing a cup of water on them to add a bit of weight. That was a trick which we had learned from a man who used to sell us turf now and again. Next morning we would bring our 'blackahs' down to Lane's or maybe Ogilvie and Moore's in Parnell Place. Most of the money thus earned we handed over to Mam, retaining only about eight pence apiece each time. That was sufficient to cover the cost of the pictures and the 'milk and odds' that night in *An Císte Milis* in Barrack Street. The glass of milk cost a penny and the odds, or cakes, were twopence each. The 'milk and odds' was as much a treat to us then as dinner in posh hotels would be today. The name *Císte Milis*, incidentally, was totally beyond Mam's comprehension and she never called it anything other than Cissie Mills.

Because so many men and women were involved in the forces England experienced an unprecedented shortage of labour. Her factories badly needed workers, her farmers urgently needed help on the land and the rich people could not get domestic staff. Because of that and also the fact that wages were higher in England than here at home many young Irish men and women left their families to avail of the opportunity of constant work over there. The only drawback was that once you got to England you were not allowed home again until the war was over. Three days a week the *Innisfallen* sailed out of Cork bound for Swansea and each day she sailed you could see scores of young men and women walking through the streets of the city on their way down to the quay to board her. The men were particularly conspicuous due to their battered old suitcases, many of which were held together with lengths of cord. Around 1941 my Uncle Sam joined the throng and went to London where a brother of his had settled many years before. Shortly afterwards my Aunt Nan also decided to go as she had lost her job in Lyons' tailoring factory owing to a slackage, but rather than follow Sam to London she went to Birmingham where she felt she might be safer and less likely to be targeted by Hitler's bombers. Their departure meant that Granda and Gran were left to fend for themselves, so it fell to us to look after them, bring them their food and fuel supply and keep their home clean and neat.

The law at the time was that the ration books of all emigrants should be returned to the Department of Industry and Commerce, Griffiths Barracks, Dublin, within four weeks of the emigrants' departure. Failure to do so resulted in severe penalties being imposed on the head of the household. Naturally everybody was most reluctant to return them hoping that their omission might not be detected and the holders could continue to draw the rations for those who had gone away. Granda decided to take the chance and retained my uncle's book. It wasn't easy to avoid detection as guards often called to homes to check the number of residents. I happened to be in Granda's shop one day when a guard called.

'Have you a son living at home with you?' he said to Granda.

'I have,' was the reply.

'Well, then, I want to speak to him,' said the guard.

It so happened that just at that very moment a funeral was passing the door. Quick as a flash Granda said: 'Oh look, there he is in the third row of men walking behind the hearse.'

The guard must have been satisfied because he took his leave and never again called looking for my uncle. Granda continued to draw the extra bit of tea and sugar until rationing ended.

Whenever he heard of someone whom he knew going to England he would make up a few packets of Mac's Smile three-hole safety razor blades and ask the emigrant to take them and post them to my uncle on reaching the shores of England. Blades were extremely difficult to get over there and their importation was strictly forbidden. Granda always knew if the blades had reached their destination because my uncle would send a letter saying: 'Mac was up last night and he made me smile.' All letters into and out of England were being censored and the reference to Mac's visit and the smile was to acknowledge receipt of the blades without the censor being any the wiser. The design on the little packets containing the blades showed a grumpy-looking man with a head as bald as an egg and a vigorous stubble of beard on his chin. The accompanying wording was as follows: 'Turn me upside down to see the effect!' Having done so you saw a man with plenty of close-cropped hair on top and a chin as smooth as silk. Even in Cork itself blades were scarce enough at that time and so men had to resharpen old ones by rubbing them up and down against the inside of a glass.

Whenever we received letters from England we sat around the fire at night and held them up to the gaslight hoping to be able to decipher those parts which had been blacked out by the censor. Of course we never succeeded. The passing weeks and months were nerve-wracking for my grandparents because one never knew when one's loved ones would fall victims to the continuous bombings. Every Friday Gran would forego her afternoon nap and walk over to the Reparation Convent in Windmill Road. Through the grille she would hand one of the nuns a half-crown and say: 'Sister, will you please light some candles before the Blessed Sacrament and ask Our Lord for protection for my sons and daughter in England?'

The Reparation Sisters were a very much loved order and throughout the day there was always one of them in silent prayer before the Blessed Sacrament.

In due course my Aunt Nan for reasons of her own moved from Birmingham to Coventry and soon after she did so we were horror-stricken to read in the *Echo* that Coventry had suffered massive air attacks. We had no way of knowing if she had survived those attacks but after a few anxious days' wait we received a letter from her reassuring us that she was all right. A large portion of the letter had been blotted out and we thought, foolishly of course, that we would be able to decipher a few words here and there. Grán was convinced that the blotted-out portion contained a message from Nan that she wished to return home. Returning was of course far easier said than done as wartime regulations did not permit it except in very extenuating circumstances. So to make Nan's homecoming possible a plot had to be conceived. The plot that was hatched necessitated Gran getting a sudden and very bad turn, so next morning she stayed in bed and word of her serious condition was dispatched to the dispensary doctor.

'How long is she like this?' he asked when he arrived.

'She got a very bad turn during the night, doctor,' Granpa said. 'She couldn't get her breath and we're very worried in case she hasn't long to live. We have a daughter over in England and you know yourself she'd love to see her before she dies. Would you ever be good enough to give us a letter to show to the guards?'

'All right so, ' he said. 'I will.'

He was as good as his word, and there and then handed a note to my mother to give to the guards stating that Gran was very seriously ill and in imminent danger of death. Shortly after his departure the 'patient' began to breathe more easily, so much so that she was able to join us around the fire that afternoon. However we knew that a guard would soon arrive to sanction my aunt's homecoming, so I was detailed to stand at the door and keep a lookout. When the guard appeared round the corner of the street I ran back into the house: 'Quick, Gran,' I said, 'there's a guard on his way up the street.' Like a flash she made a dash for the stairs and rushed up those steps as never before, kicked off her shoes and dived fully clothed under the bed-clothes. As the guard entered her bedroom she was panting and almost completely out of breath. One look at her satisfied him that she was indeed in a serious condition. He promptly sanctioned my aunt's return, and so a telegram was sent off to Coventry. The message was brief: 'Come quick, mother dying'. Nan was understandably shocked on receiving the telegram and arranged to travel as soon as ever possible. She arrived two days later, tired and weary after a worrying sea-journey and an unbelievable fourteen hour train journey from Dublin to Cork. As she rushed at the door her first words were: 'Is she dead?' On being told that Gran was indeed alive and kicking she dashed in to find her sitting in comfort beside the fire. They both burst into tears of relief as they hugged and embraced one another. When the excitement subsided somewhat Nan had the details of the plot explained to her. It was then that she came to realise the extent to which her parents feared for her safety in Coventry.

After a brisk exchange of news and stories Nan opened her case and placed on the table four loaves of beautiful white bread, a tin of spam and a packet of dried egg-powder. Straight away we began to devour the bread so eagerly that one could be forgiven for thinking that we hadn't had a meal for days. The fact however was that we hadn't seen such white bread since the outbreak of hostilities. The spam did not taste at all to our liking, and as for the egg-powder, when Nan informed us that one mixed it with water and then fried it we almost got sick on the spot. Retiring to the corner she let down her stocking revealing a large bandage on her shin. Then she removed the bandage and around the floor fell what could only be described as a cascade of notes which exceeded many times the ten pounds maximum which a person was at that time allowed to take out of England. Our Nan was no fool. She hadn't got her head for a hat, and so she successfully got the money through the customs barrier. Obviously the officer was not very strict, but nevertheless he had a sense of humour because on examining the document that showed the reason for her being allowed home he remarked sardonically: 'There's no war in Ireland, yet there are more people dying there than in the whole of Russia!'

The war continued on week by week, month by month, and despite our country's policy of neutrality it seemed at times inevitable that we would become embroiled in it, but thank God that never happened. Maybe the Lord felt that we had already experienced our own share of fighting during the 1919s and the 1920s. Times were tough and certain commodities were scarce, yet on reflection one cannot fail to realise that there existed during the war years a civic spirit which was a credit to our people. After all our state was still very young, a mere twenty years or so of age, but our government and our people displayed a maturity and a determination of which they could justifiably be very proud.

SEE YOU INSIDE

Being a wage-earner brought with it a certain amount of independence and also the much desired privilege of being allowed to attend late shows in the cinemas. The best loved, largest and most elegant cinema in Cork was the Savoy in Patrick Street which opened its doors to the public for the first time in 1931. Its beautifully cushioned seats and padded arm-rests were indeed a far cry from the wooden seats that we were previously accustomed to in Miah's or the Assembly Rooms. The Savoy was the only cinema which provided entertainment in which the patrons could take an active part. That came before each screening of the film. Rising as it were out of the bowels of the auditorium the massive multi-coloured organ would appear, the lights dimmed and a spotlight focused on the organist Fred Bridgeman resplendent in a monkey-suit and seated at the keyboard. A great cheer from the patrons welcomed Fred, who would then swivel around to acknowledge the audience's welcome before starting to provide a spirited rendering of the popular songs of the day. The words were flashed on the screen and the audience joined in the singing. The older people derived great enjoyment from the sing-song but not so much the younger ones who had little time for the mushy sentiments of Frank Sinatra and Bing Crosby. At the completion of the sing-song the smiling sleek-haired bespectacled Fred would rise from his stool, turn round, face the audience and gracefully bow to them before disappearing down into the nether regions from which he had earlier risen.

Going to the various cinemas gave us young girls, the 'dolls', the opportunity of tangling with the boys, especially the 'gawzers'. They were the good-looking fellows, and a favourite saying of the girls whenever they espied a gawzer was: 'Would you look at him? Isn't he a smasher? Sure you'd smudder your mudder for him!'

Many of the fellows whom we used to come across in the

cinemas were young lads who had just left school and were in dead-end jobs as messenger-boys delivering goods by bicycle to the homes of customers of the larger shops. Their pay was minimal and the only perk available was that some shop-owners allowed the boys to keep the bicycle at home some weekends.

Those boys were at the stage where their interest in us girls was quickly increasing, and sure enough we were not slow in reciprocating. What is natural cannot be wondered at, but they pretended to be tough and wouldn't make any move until the lights in the cinema went out and the show began. Then they would take leave of their companions and scrush their way in beside a girl who had already taken their eye while the lights were on. If the film was a rather frightening, one such as those featuring Boris Karloff, the boy would take hold of the girl's hand at a suitably terrifying moment as if to reassure her that there was no need to panic. If she didn't reject him he would, with growing confidence, stretch his arm around the back of the seat and rest it on her shoulders. All going well he might whisper into her ear just before the conclusion of the film: 'Will you be at the Col tomorrow night?'

The Col was short for the Coliseum Cinema at the east end of MacCurtain Street. The building has long since ceased to be a cinema and now houses the Coliseum Sports Bowl. If the girl agreed he would then reply: 'All right so. I'll see you inside.'

There was no question of meeting her outside. Financial stringencies were such that he couldn't afford to pay for her, and she understood his predicament. Such budding romances seldom endured but they served the purpose of adding a bit of harmless spice to young lives. There was one particular messenger boy who was extremely popular with the girls, not because of his looks or charming manner or engaging conversation but because he worked in a confectioner's shop and always went to the cinema with bait in the form of a bagful of white icing which by the time he took up his seat would have become rock-hard. Sitting next to him the lucky girl munched her way all through the picture, and hard though that icing might be she appreciated it just as much in those war years as her counterpart today would appreciate a box of the most exquisite handmade chocolates. Other commodities were available too, depending on where the boys worked. I recall getting a tube of Tattoo lipstick from one who was employed in a leading chemist's shop. It was a very expensive type and though he never said as much it was more than likely that, shall I say, it hadn't gone through the books. I was thrilled with it, of course, but I couldn't tell my mother as she strongly disapproved of lipstick, so I kept it hidden inside the lining at the lower corner of my coat, later to be withdrawn and used only when I was safely outside the door.

The messenger boys and other young lads like them never gave us girls any trouble. The older men were the ones to beware of, and parents repeatedly warned their daughters not to sit next to any of them on their own. Those fellows were usually on the prowl and deserved their reputation of being dirty old men.

By degrees I was getting my eye-teeth and looking forward to proceeding further than the cinema. The next step was the Opera House but that posed a financial problem because while one could get into the cinemas for as little as three pence the cheapest seats in the Opera House up high in the 'gods' cost all of nine pence, which required having a reasonably good job or failing that, a boyfriend who could afford to bring you with him. Even the poor of Cork loved the Opera House where they could enjoy the real thing as it were, German massed bands, Russian ballet and drama and opera companies. They always tried to be present for opening nights, no matter what the cost.

Cork always had, and still has, a great opera tradition. It was nothing new to hear the older people rendering arias at even the humblest of parties while messenger boys travelling round the city on their bikes whistled *Home to our Mountains* and other such popular pieces. Can Cork people really be blamed then for feeling that they possess that extra little bit of class? They like to think that there are professors amongst them who never darkened the doors of the university.

I am told that the first ever visit by a Russian ballet company created quite a stir. In those days puritanism was alive and well in Cork as elsewhere, manifesting itself in many ways, particularly with regard to dress. Old women wore their clothes right down to their ankles and even young girls dared not venture forth in dresses so short that their knees were visible. Not surprisingly then, when it was announced that Russian ballet dancers were coming to the Opera House some citizens became alarmed at the prospect of scantily clad females flinging their arms and legs about on the stage. More alarming still was the thought of shaped-out male dancers cavorting in dress that revealed all too faithfully the contours of their anatomy, particularly certain parts thereof! So when the idea of a protest march to the Opera House on opening night was floated it met with enthusiastic support from both the women and men of the city. The marchers – all of them men because the prevailing custom was that women did not participate in public marches – assembled and headed for the Opera House. They arrived well before the show was due to begin. Meanwhile, however, word was passed backstage to the Russians that the march was under way, but for some unknown reason – perhaps it was due to a problem in communication – the Russians understood that the march was one of welcome, so they promptly appeared outside on the steps of the Opera House to acknowledge the wonderful gesture. Confusion ensued and the protest turned out to be a damp squib. The protesters' ardour cooled, the people in general later relented and the day finally came when Cork could proudly boast of its own ballet company.

The first dance I ever attended was a weekly céilí and old-time in St Francis Hall in Sheares' Street, now part of a licensed premises. Dancing hours for our age-group were from four o'clock to six on Sunday afternoons. One can only imagine how the young girls of the present day would react were it suggested to them that they go to a dance at four on a Sunday afternoon, and yet it is extremely doubtful whether they enjoy themselves one whit more than we did. A boy next door brought his sister and myself along to the hall and gave us every second dance. Thankfully I mastered the intricacies of the dances in a short space of time and could never be numbered amongst the 'leggers', those poor girls who had no sense of rhythm, found it difficult to learn how to dance and were all too often consigned to the role of wallflowers. If a boy or girl wished to have lessons before venturing out to the dance-halls, and had the money to pay for them, then Nanette's on the Grand Parade was the place to go. Nanette, though small in stature, was nevertheless physically well-endowed. She would wind up the gramophone and play a waltz of bygone days to begin with. If you had no partner she would guide your faltering steps around the room, and if there was another learner present she would give him or her a brush with which to practise.

The nuns in St Vincent's Convent on St Mary's Road ran dances for young boys and girls in their hall known as the Oratory, but one had always to be on one's best behaviour there. Even the slightest suggestion of hanky-panky was out of the question as a nun went around the hall during each dance with a twelve-inch ruler in her hand measuring the distance between the dancing partners. Twelve inches was the shortest distance permissible and anyone exceeding the limit was suitably reprimanded and advised not to re-offend. At the interval a decade of the Rosary was recited. Consequently those who might have had any ideas about cheek-to-cheek dancing or a little touch of closeness forgot about the hall and sought their pleasures elsewhere. I am told that nowadays you couldn't get the thickness of a ruler, never mind its length, between some couples. Amongst the other venues that catered for would-be Fred Astaires were the Thomas Ashe Memorial Hall on Fr Mathew Quay, MacCurtain Hall at the bottom of Shandon Street, the Old Maids' down in Tivoli, and the Reds and Whites in Douglas Village. The Central Ballroom on the North Jetty was frequented mostly by foreigners while Mac's on the South Jetty was the soldiers' Mecca. Both were absolutely out of bounds for girls of my age, however, as our parents would not countenance our having anything to do with foreigners or soldiers. Fraternising with the latter was frowned upon for no reason other than a prejudice against the uniform which had been handed down since the days of the British army and particularly the Black and Tans.

The dances in all those venues finished at eleven o'clock except, perhaps, on special occasions such as St Stephen's Night, New Year's Eve and St Patrick's Night when there was an extension to one or two o'clock in the morning. On one particular St Stephen's Night I was granted permission to go to a late dance at the Reds and Whites which cost sixpence. That was a new departure, indeed a milestone in my life, and I felt I had finally come of age. It proved to be a wonderful night. The Rinso was scattered on the floor as usual to make it slippery, and the band consisting of an accordionist, a fiddler and a drummer played their hearts out. It was heaven, the night flew and so enthralled was I that I missed the last bus home. A gallant young man with whom I had a couple of dances became aware of my predicament and kindly offered me a lift on his bicycle. I naturally presumed that he was going to give me a 'crosser' on the crossbar but then I learned that his was a lady's bike and I would have to sit on the handlebars, not by a long shot the most comfortable means of transport. Nevertheless it was much better than walking. Up I went on the handlebars and so with me leaning back against him and my legs dangling on either side of the front wheel my young Lochinvar brought me the full length of the Douglas Road and up home to Greenmount. Years upon years had elapsed before I met him again. He was home on holidays from London. Naturally the conversation turned to our younger days: 'Do you remember,' he said, 'the night long ago I conveyed you home from the Reds and Whites on the handlebars of a bike?'

'Of course I do,' I said, 'and I was most grateful for it. Wasn't it a great night too?'

'It was,' he said, 'but one thing you didn't know was that I took that bicycle without permission from outside a house near the hall. Fair dues to me, though, I returned it after taking you home.'

On many occasions since then I have asked myself who am I to talk about joyriders. Maybe I was the original joyrider because if that same situation had arisen in modern times that chap might have stolen a car to take me home! But then again I know he would never have damaged or crashed it.

The finest and best loved dance-hall in Cork was the Arc, or to give it its full title the Arcadia Ballroom, just across from the gate of Kent Railway Station, but the entrance fee, while not exorbitant, was such that the likes of me could not afford it and so we had to wait for a significant increase in wages before getting to see the inside of it. Interestingly enough soldiers in uniform were not admitted to the Arc. There was, however, another dancehall which could be described as the intermediate stage between the smaller ones which we first frequented and the spacious Arc. That was the Gresham Rooms in Maylor Street but even that was beyond me financially until I received a rise in wages at Dwyers. The Gresham was very popular with the country boys who on Sunday nights cycled in. Apart altogether from their accent which differed quite considerably from that of the city lads they were instantly recognisable by the yellow cable-stitch hand-knitted pullovers which most of them sported. As for the various dances themselves the popularity poll at that time was headed by the veleta, with the military two-step and the old-time waltz following closely behind. The jitterbugging craze had just hit Ireland but that was frowned upon in the Gresham and anyone trying to introduce it was promptly ordered off the floor and barred from the hall.

When the time arrived that we had the wherewithal to pay our way into the Arcadia our happiness knew no bounds but on occasions such as St Stephen's Night so many people went dancing that it was impossible to get into either it or the Gresham Rooms, and so we resorted to the country halls. On such occasions we were conveyed in special buses from Parnell Place. We liked to think that with our fancy dresses, our lipstick and our high heels we made quite an impression on the country boys on their own stamping ground. In those dancehalls, and indeed in the city halls also, the girls all sat or stood at one side while the boys were ranged across from them on the other. During the interval between dances the boys cast furtive eyes across at the girls sizing them up, especially the new 'talent', and then as soon as the band struck up the music for the next dance they dashed across and whisked the girl of their choice on to the floor. For some reason we always found the country boys that bit more difficult to handle than their city counterparts but girls always gave one another total support and were well capable of handling any situation.

The leading hotels of the city catered for the dancing fraternity by holding an occasional ball. The most famous of all was undoubtedly the Pluckers' Ball which was held in the Imperial Hotel in the month of January each year. At that time hundreds of young girls were employed as pluckers by the many fowl-exporting companies operating in Cork, and were obliged to work under adverse and inhospitable conditions in cold sheds in the Marsh, Tower Street and other areas also. Coming up to the busy Christmas season many temporary pluckers were taken on to help supply Irish and English homes with the traditional turkey or goose. These temporary workers were almost invariably married women who themselves, and more than likely their mothers before them, had worked as pluckers prior to marriage, and went back to earn a few extra pounds for Christmas. The pluckers were a cheery bunch in spite of the drudgery of the work and the long hours which often meant not finishing until well into the night. During the war years they had to undergo what was to them the eerie experience of walking home through the pitch-black city streets because of the government-imposed ban on public lighting, known generally as the blackout. That was a measure intended to avoid Irish cities and towns being subjected to bomb attacks by German planes. Such a situation would not, of course, have presented any problem to country girls who were well accustomed to venturing out on dark nights, but that was of little consolation to the pluckers, and so in order to allay their fear of the darkness they would tightly link arms and walk in lines stretching right across the width of the street.

The pluckers, even those only fourteen or fifteen years of age, all wore black shawls, and one could not mistake them at least by day, because the shawls, covered as they inevitably were in tiny specks of fine white down, betrayed them. Their hair also had a liberal covering of down, and seeing a dark-haired girl with her hair dotted with the soft white flecks was like seeing a Russian Princess 'whose tresses an ermine cape adorned'. Come the night of the Plucker's Ball, however, these self-same ladies were resplendent in evening dresses and ball-gowns of the finest fashion. It was as if some fairy godmother had transformed their appearance.

EACH ELM TREE

Girls and boys began 'sparking' or walking out – the word 'courting' was not part of our vocabulary – at the age of fourteen or fifteen. It was really harmless carry-on, certainly by today's standards. Patrick Street was a great place to meet members of the opposite sex. One never went on one's own but rather as a member of a group, hunting in droves, as you might say. Those groups strolling up and down on the lookout were in Cork terminology said to be 'doing Pana', but this activity was confined almost completely to the southern side of the street around Woolworths. The northern side was rarely resorted to. Two or three girls might saunter slowly along past a group of boys talking and chatting by the kerb. It was strategically important that the sauntering be done at the proper pace, leisurely and not too hurried, otherwise the wrong signals might be sent out. One of the boys with puckered lips might say something which sounded like 'Cush! Cush!' That would be followed by the opening salvo: 'Me ould dote yeh, if I had the money I'd court yeh!' It was the turn of one of the girls then to come up with the standard reply: 'And if I had a gun I'd shoot yeh!' But a girl on her own wouldn't have the courage to stop and would scuttle past the boys with blushing cheeks and bowed head.

The ice was by now broken and the girls would continue sauntering along for a few paces as if to give the impression that they were still involved in the process of making up their minds how to react. It would not do to appear too willing. Playing ever so slightly hard-to-get was the preferable option but it was only a ploy, as the boys knew very well. Gradually the two groups sidled up to one another and began to chat but soon a boy and girl would move away a yard or two and then the chatting-up commenced, shyly at first perhaps. If all went well and they were both agreeable a date was made to meet the following night. That would as likely as not mean a walk up the Mardyke which in those times of paltry wages cost nothing. The secluded Dyke was close to the city, yet it boasted of two rows of mature elm trees and no traffic other than bikes, an idyllic setting for romantically inclined youth. On the following night it was, of course, important to take the wise precaution of not being late in reaching the Dyke lest all the trees be taken up by other courting couples and where was one to go then? People still recall the time when consternation was caused among the Dyke's young patrons on discovering that the trunk of every tree had been tarred up to a height of six or seven feet. The perpetrators were never found out though some people believed that the priests were responsible but that was mere speculation. There were, however, many of the younger citizens of Cork who firmly believed that a more ulterior and spoilsport motive prompted on the Corporation's part was responsible. Anyhow the Dyke was never the same afterwards and in due course lost its appeal for those seeking to experience love's young dream.

Cáit Shea's Lane was another famous place for sparking couples, but was mainly patronised by boys and girls living in the western suburbs, because in those days, or should I say nights, any place west of Dennehy's Cross was to city people the equivalent of Land's End. Hangdog Road on the Southside was much more convenient to our area, and was considered to be the most suitable walking-out area of all. On one side of the road were the market gardens and the many gates leading into them but the other side provided a liberal supply of stalling places along the green mossy bank. Those sections of the bank where a couple could sit down were in great demand and as with the Mardyke's elm trees early booking was advisable. Otherwise couples had to resort to those stalls which offered standing room only. On summer evenings bowling matches were played on Hangdog Road but the players and the spectators with great understanding ignored the young couples involved in less strenuous activity, whereas on winter nights the place was dead quiet with no passers-by except for the odd man out exercising his dog.

When going out on a jag – we rarely used the word 'date' – the boys and girls tried to look their best and thus create a good impression. Some boys displayed a tendency to overuse brilliantine on their hair. Brilliantine was available in small thin bottles and cost two pence, the cheapest of the cheap. The smell of it matched the price. The more they put on their hair the more handsome they seemed to think it made them. Sometimes it ran down their necks, and if those same necks weren't as clean as they might be then the streaks showed up like high-water marks on the strand.

Girls preparing for a jag and in whose homes there was no bath would have a 'dive in the dish' and wash themselves thoroughly with strong carbolic soap, paying particular attention to the 'gink', or face. In very cold weather the dive in the dish meant washing one half of the body one week and the other half the following week. Washing one's face in flake-meal applied with a cloth was considered excellent for the skin. If a girl wished to wear make-up a visit to the cosmetic counter in Woolworth's was undertaken. There she could purchase for twopence a small capsule of Outdoor Girl lipstick. The number on the capsule indicated the shade. Number Seven was a brilliant red, Number Six was of orange hue and Number Four was pink. Outdoor Girl and Pond's face-powders could be bought for sixpence while a base for the powder packed in small tins set you back a further fourpence. If you really wanted to splash out and hope to reap the dividend you bought a scent of some sort for a further fourpence. The most popular of these came in a small dark-blue bottle and prided itself in the romantic name of 'Evening in Paris'. What an evening in Paris had that an evening in Cork did not have we never could find out.

It was the ambition of every girl to have high-heeled shoes and silk stockings. Whereas the older generation mostly wore lisle stockings we were interested only in pure silk ones, in particular the Green Valley brand manufactured here in Blackpool by Sunbeam Wolsey, but they cost seven shillings and sixpence, a daunting sum of money in those days, and if a girl couldn't afford them her only hope was that her boyfriend might find it in his heart to buy her a pair as a present. In the summertime – and we did get really fine summers then – there was no need of stockings because we could invest in a bottle of Miner's Liquid Tan which we rubbed on our legs. The most widely used shade was Sun Haze. Girls who hadn't the price of the tan or a pair of stockings made do with a concoction of their own consisting of turf ash mixed with water. However the main drawback of the latter was that if a girl wearing it was caught in a sudden shower of rain of the type which we often experience during summer in Ireland the tan ran down her legs leaving in its train streaks of various shades of light brown, a sight not calculated to allure the boys. Of hair-shampoo we knew nothing but we had our own home-made product to give our hair a lovely sheen. It consisted of vinegar mixed with water. I clearly recall washing my hair with it before going to a dance one night. We were dancing out in the middle of the floor when my partner remarked: 'There's an awful smell of fish and chips somewhere!' I pretended to be suitably surprised but did not make him any the wiser as to its origin, and if he became aware of it he was gentlemanly enough not to mention it again. Toothpaste was another commodity which we did not possess simply because we hadn't the money to buy it, so we used salt instead and applied it to our teeth with a clean piece of cloth. For special occasions soot was recommended. Contradictory though it may seem it made teeth pearly white.

After a few months of steady courtship a boy might perhaps give his girlfriend a present, not a very dear one though. The gesture, not the cost of the present, was the important thing. I remember one occasion when the chap I was going with won some money on a horse so he splashed out and bought me a Celtic Cross on a chain. He thought it was brilliant and so did I, but after a short time a green line around my neck indicated the inferior quality of the cross and I had to discard it forthwith. Mothers who had marriageable daughters and were anxious about their financial well-being after marriage always advised them to concentrate their efforts on tradesmen because tradesmen for the most part had regular work and were able to command a higher wage than any other section of the workforce. However, things did not always turn out as mothers planned because, human nature being what it is, if a girl met a chap who was kind, considerate and affectionate she mightn't stop to think of assessing his potential as a provider. Not all young girls were as coldly calculating as their mothers might wish, and that in itself was no bad thing.

After perhaps a year's courtship the girl would bring the boy home to meet her mother who, if she approved, would do all in her power to show he was welcome and make him feel at home. The currant cake and other goodies were provided with a view to making a good impression and so began the tightening of the noose. Every mother was most anxious to see her daughters getting married and settling down at a young age. Not only was she pleased to have them off her hands, but it also meant that there was no danger of what was euphemistically described as her 'getting into trouble'. Such a misfortune often caused serious spleens and fighting with a girl's father and brothers. Sometimes they would try to wreak revenge on the man responsible. If he wished to marry her he might grudgingly be allowed to do so, and in such a situation the marriage took place at the back of the altar and there was no Mass. If he wasn't prepared to marry her he might risk staying around or if the heat was getting too great he might depart the scene altogether and sail away to England on the *Innisfallen*.

Sex education for young girls was non-existent save for whatever the birds and the bees might teach them, and few houses had either an aviary or an apiary! Mothers, not to mention fathers, never discussed the facts of life with their daughters, and the only advice given amounted to: 'Mind yourself. Be careful when you go out and be back at eleven.'

The girls themselves were no fools and had their own simple but nevertheless effective ways of ensuring that a boy's intentions were serious and honourable. They might be the weaker sex but they knew full well how to soften a boy's cough for him or play the old soldier, and lead him a merry dance. Not turning up for a date, usually described as giving him a fifty, could also teach him a salutary though sometimes undeserved lesson. Alternatively a girl might go walking out with a fellow for a while, and if it seemed to her that he was becoming rather interested she would drop him for a while and go walking out with another. Then if the first fellow continued to chase her she felt she had sufficient grounds for doubting him no longer. Boys were naive enough and easier to snare then than nowadays.

The majority of girls, like myself, were married by the age of twenty. In fact I know a few who took the plunge at sixteen. Girls and boys began sparking at a young age, and because of the size of families and the lack of room in the houses it made sense that sons and daughters leave the nest early on. When a couple decided that they wished to marry the boy would propose to the girl and if she were agreeable to an engagement he would buy the ring. Presumably each boy had his own way of proposing. Some of them were reputed to do so by asking such questions as 'Can I hang up my shirt on the line next to your undies?' or 'Would you like to be buried with my people?' The latter form was unlikely to meet with approval in the city as girls would have their own ideas as to where she might wish her bones to rest when that hopefully far-off event had to be faced.

Many stories are related of girls who purposely threw their engagement rings over Patrick's Bridge into the Lee after a lover's tiff. A newly engaged couple whom I knew had just acquired a house and as they were returning home one night they had a difference of opinion, to put it mildly, which resulted in the girl removing the ring from her finger and throwing

136

it over the garden wall of a nearby house. In an attempt to humiliate him further – it was all a pretence of course – she told him to go and look for it if he wished. But he was made of sterner stuff than she realised and vehemently refused to do so. The game was up, she quickly repented and knocked on the door of the house in question. When the lady of the house appeared the girl, by this time in a suitably chastened and re-pentant mood, explained her predicament and asked if she would help her in the search. She readily agreed to do so. A light of some sort was obviously necessary but torches were rare and the street lighting was almost non-existent. However with the aid of a bundle of lighting papers the ring was found and promptly restored to its rightful place on the girl's finger.

Accommodation-hunting was the next item on the agenda. It was, as they used to say, the boy's job to put a home around the girl. They would go looking for a room or two in a tene-ment, particularly if either his or her mother was already living in one. The mother would know of any tenant who had died or moved out, and would immediately approach the landlady on behalf of the young couple. If the mother was known to be a good payer the landlady was only too glad to accede to her request. Families were very closely knit so the idea of the young couple and the old couple living in the same house had a great appeal. If on the other hand a small house became available the couple might opt for it, but that happened only rarely.

The girl's parish priest had to be given due notice of the impending nuptials. If he was fond of money he might say to the girl: 'Have five pounds in an envelope for me the morning I marry you.' There was a extended family in the city and a few became priests. They were noted for their love of money. One of them married this particular couple and having performed the ceremony he held out his hand for the envelope. It was readily handed over by the groom but the priest on opening it found it contained just a ten-shilling note. He challenged the groom about being shortchanged but the only satisfaction he got was: 'The job is done now, Father, and you can't undo it. That's all you're getting, and you can take it or leave it.'

The practice of giving wedding presents was not at all as widespread as it is today. The mother of either the bride or the groom, depending on their respective financial situations, supplied a double bed, while close relatives or friends might give pairs of sheets, pillow slips, clocks, ornaments, pictures, statues of the Infant of Prague, half-sets of ware, pots or perhaps overmantel mirrors. There were no fancy presents. Everything could be put to practical use.

The bride-to-be, if in employment, continued to work up to the very last day before the wedding because every pound was important. When finally the big day came the couple arrived at the church in time for Mass and Nuptial Blessing. That could be at seven or eight or maybe nine o'clock in the morning. After Mass they went to the bride's home to a party which lasted all day. Both families, as well as some friends and neighbours, were invited. The spread didn't have to be very elaborate and twenty pounds was normally sufficient to cover the cost of a ham, a bit of pork perhaps, lots of cakes, a tierce of porter and a bottle of whiskey. Then as the night wore on and the drop of drink went to their heads the company became merry and the desire to parade their vocal talents was all-consuming. Arias from the operas were the choice of most performers. A small insignificant little fellow might stick out his chest, tilt back his head and launch into 'Let Me like a Soldier Fall'. Another might give a droolly rendering of 'Your Tiny Hand is Frozen'. Everyone had his or her own special song and nobody else trespassed on their territory.

Going on the honeymoon most likely meant travelling to Youghal for the day if it was summertime, whereas if it was a winter wedding they went home that night to their own house or rooms and slept there. On the morning after the wedding more likely than not the bride's mother, being solicitous for her daughter's welfare, called to see her. She would ask no questions, but simply wished to be reassured that she was 'all right'.

Discerning readers will have little difficulty in understanding the reason for the mother's anxiety. Curiously enough it was presumed that there was no danger of the bridegroom having being adversely affected overnight.

The first year of marriage was heaven for the young bride. She had given up her job and so no more had she to rush through the streets to work in the early morning. Every husband liked to convey the notion that he could support his wife on his own income and a working wife was tantamount to an admission of failure in that regard. It made him feel less of a man. The wife used the situation to her advantage and so she dawdled leisurely through the day. She might saunter off down town in the morning or visit her married friends or go to a matinée in the afternoon. However that year of bliss soon passed and then as the children came along she was obliged to face the realities of family life, and in later years she might seek a few days' work in one of the city's big houses to supplement her husband's income.

From the day of the wedding onwards the bride's mother never made mention of pregnancy or any related matters. When in God's own time it became obvious that the girl was pregnant she was advised to stay at home as much as possible, and should she decide to come back to visit her family occasionally her mother was at pains to get her out of the house again before her unmarried brothers of whatever age arrived. Alternatively she might throw an old curtain or some similar material over her to cover up the bulge because 'your brothers will be in soon'. It was vulgar to be seen to be in the family way. Little wonder then that the mother was usually the last to be informed of a pregnancy. The expectant girl was far more likely to confide in a married friend of her own age.

Within a few months of the young girl's wedding the old women of the neighbourhood would start sizing her up, particularly from the side, and watching for any of the tell-tale symptoms. So sharp and eagle-eyed were they that they knew she was expecting almost as soon as she herself did. 'Any news?' was the usual question. Some of them maintained that the look in the girl's eyes was what gave the game away. In any case as soon as they had verification of the girl's pregnancy, though in their language she was not pregnant, but 'on the way' or 'for the road', they gave advice freely. 'You'd want to eat up now, girl. You're eating for two, you know!'

Then shortly before the baby was due, and all the time aware that she could expect little advice from her mother, they would try to ease her fears, particularly if she was expecting for the first time, and reassuringly they would say: 'Don't be worried now, girl. A dose of castor oil and 'twill be all over in a few minutes.' If after a few years of married life the young woman showed no signs of anything doing the more serious-minded would look upon it as God's will but that God was good and would put things right in his own time. Some of the more roguish-minded friends, however, might advise the husband to put his hat on 'the next time', or the wife to eat more duck eggs.

The Erinville on Western Road catered for all the women who wished to give birth to their children in hospital. At one stage it had just forty beds and that was more than sufficient for the number of expectant mothers who wished to avail of its services. Indeed Nurse Maggie Long, who 'borned' all my own children, once told me that when she was training in the Erinville around the year 1915 she was let go for a spell, her services not being required due to business being slack. Whether the slackage was due to the number of mothers who wished to give birth at home or to a certain inaction on the part of their husbands I cannot say.

Each dispensary district had its own midwife. Nurse Hosford, a Protestant woman who lived on French's Quay, worked in my mother's area. She was a most popular person who always dressed in a navy blue cape, and on her head wore a frill of lace from which a navy blue veil hung down her back. Maggie Long who lived in Blarney Street did trojan work as a midwife in the north side of the city. During the period usually referred to as 'The Troubles' in the late 1919s and early 1920s she was required to have a permit to answer nightcalls during curfew. Those two midwives and many others like them were on call every hour seven days a week with never a complaint and snatching sleep whenever they could. They tended rich and poor alike, borning babies of the better-off in the dearest and finest of sheets as well as the babies of the poor who entered the world with nothing under them only copies of the *Echo*. Is it any wonder that Cork people have such a love of reading?

When an expectant mother felt her labour pains begin she would gently break the news to her husband with the words: 'I think I'm for it tonight.'

Then he would turn around and say innocently: 'Maybe 'tis something you ate!'

A neighbour might come in and sit beside the mother-to-be until it was time to send for the midwife. When the midwife arrived she took over. The husband wasn't made any the wiser as to how matters were proceeding nor did he display any great desire to know. He shied away from it all. He might dash out the door at the first inkling of the impending arrival and walk up and down outside, a fumbling bundle of nerves, until he heard the baby crying and knew that the matter was over and done with. Even if he made it known that he would like to be present for the big occasion the midwife would give him short shrift and tell him be off about his business. There was a mystery about women then which has now been lost and I consider that a great pity even though I fully appreciate the desire of many modern fathers to be present at the birth of their offspring.

The midwife stayed on until mother and child were absolutely safe and well and for seven days afterwards she visited them twice a day, bathed the baby, tended the mother and went to the chemist's shop to buy any medicine that might be required. She provided a truly all-in service. When the day came for the child to be baptised – and that was invariably in

141

the first week of its life – she dressed it up in all its finery and carried it in her arms to the church, together with the father and sponsors or 'gossips'. Later she registered the child in the local dispensary. In the 1950s all that devoted care and attention cost the parents a mere two pounds and ten shillings. Even if costs in general have rocketed skywards since then and medical science has improved out of all recognition still I never cease to be horrified when I hear of women nowadays paying hundreds and hundreds of pounds to have their babies in hospital.

As soon as all the hullabuloo was over and the mother had recovered the husband was more often than not back in bed again with his wife because there was nowhere else for him to sleep unless he resorted to the floor and that was not an inviting prospect. Such a situation inevitably brought its own problems. There was no such thing as contraception or birth control – people hadn't even heard of the words – and under those circumstances it is not surprising that many a young mother had a baby every year or two. She might complain about her plight during pregnancy but the moment she held the new arrival in her arms she would gladly give all she possessed to ensure that nothing untoward would ever befall the child.

If, as often happened, the couple couldn't afford to buy a cot, or indeed if a second one was needed, the simplest means of solving the problem was to get an orange-box. This measured approximately three feet by one and a half. The dividing piece in the middle was removed and the bottom and sides of the box were padded with a nice soft cloth. The improvised cot was then placed on two chairs beside the bed so that the baby was within easy reach of the mother. A severe lack of space sometimes dictated that babies sleep in an open drawer, and there is no evidence to suggest that such humble beginnings did them any harm or set them back in any way.

The last child of a family, often described as the last of the litter or the scrapings of the pot, might be rather delicate, and perhaps underweight initially. In such a case the child was kept in its cradle near the fire and was never washed with water but cleansed with olive oil to preserve its body heat. The baby was dressed in a white or red flannel vest designed to keep the chest warm as the common belief was that most ailments in young children stemmed from the chest. Liquid paraffin was relied upon to clear up many complaints, and magnesia was administered if yellow jaundice made its appearance. A child given such loving care and attention was said to be 'reared out of the fire'. All children, whether healthy or otherwise, were breast-fed but if for some reason that was not possible they were fed only cow's milk until such time as they were well able to walk. The first solid food they received was a mixture of warm milk and bread with a sprinkling of sugar. This was known almost universally as 'goody'. There was also 'tea-goody' which consisted of milky tea, bread and sugar. The main criticism that might be made of such a diet was that it left children over-susceptible to rickets. To soothe a cross child some of the old women resorted to what can only be described as an unorthodox remedy. They would put their first finger on their tongue to moisten it, then dip it in the sugar and push it into the child's mouth. Some of those same women used snuff so one can only wonder what the resultant concoction tasted like.

It was common practice that once a child had acquired some teeth it was given a crubeen bone to suck. This was not as outrageous or as unhygienic as it might seem to people nowadays, for the simple reason that a crubeen bone, when all the meat has been removed from it, is very clean and very smooth and would not cut the gums. Of course the child had to be big enough to be capable of handling the bone without assistance.

DAUGHTERS OF EVE

Some husbands cherished the belief that they were the boss in the home and the women were quite happy not to disillusion them. They used their heads when dealing with their husbands and had the gift of being able to make them think that they were in charge. Even when it came down to buying an item of clothing a wife might say, in deference to her husband as it were, 'John, I think I'll buy that.' That was the beginning of the softening-up process. She would bide her time then and when the opportune moment came, perhaps some night after he had a few drinks, she would return to the subject again, as if in all innocence: 'John, do you remember I was saying I'd like to buy a frock?' In his weak moment he would say: 'Right, Mary. Go on away and buy it.' What John didn't realise, of course, was that Mary had already bought it and hidden it away safely from his gaze.

When I got married I was the recipient of much advice from older women in the neighbourhood. On the first such occasion that I recall an old woman, a veteran of the vicissitudes of married life, took me aside.

'Listen here to me now, girl,' she said. 'Do you know what I says to every girl that gets married? If he's good to you, you be good to him too, and halve your heart with him, and if there's only two rashers in the house give him one and have one yourself. But if he's not good to you wait till the hoor is gone out and eat the two yourself.'

The following was the advice another old woman proferred me as to how to avoid undue pressure of work.

'Don't ever pretend that you're strong. Let on that your chest isn't good and that the smell of paint and things like that don't agree with you. If you're too willing when you get married first he'll let you do the painting and other jobs, so be a little on the weak side and you'll get away with a lot.'

Then there was the other seasoned campaigner who advised me on how to deal effectively with a husband who might be reluctant to part with his money even to feed the children.

'Watch him closely,' she said, 'and follow his movements. They all have places where they plank the money. Most of them plank it under a loose floorboard upstairs, so when he's up there on his own have your ear cocked and when he's gone out you go upstairs, lift up the lino, look for the loose floorboard and you have him. Or if he comes in after a bout of drinking raid his pockets because when he sobers up he won't remember what he did with the money. Then when he goes back to the plank again the next day and finds no money he'll be thinking did he spend it all last night. You have him then because if he says there's money gone out of his pocket you just say: "No wonder there is, because you drank it all last night!" So he'll keep his mouth shut for he won't give you the satisfaction of admitting that he was on the ran-tan-tan.'

There were, of course, some women who were too timid or didn't possess the necessary guile or courage to assert themselves and so had to endure a hard life at the hands of their husbands, but by and large the women had a devilish side to their character if they chose to use it. This enabled them to bamboozle men without the men ever realising it. It must be that Eve's brain was superior to that of Adam! I doubt, however, if that is true today because television and the media in general concentrate too much on women and analyse them to such an extent that all their little secrets are revealed, they have lost the edge on the men and the advantage which they once enjoyed over them is now no more.

Men would never contemplate having a drink at home unless there was a party of some sort, and that was indeed a rarity. They much preferred the atmosphere of the pub. Rarely if ever would young women dream of entering a pub. That would be frowned upon, and even on the odd occasion when some of the older women went out for a drink they never appeared in the public bar but resorted to the snug where they could avoid the public gaze and also any rough conversation that some of the men might indulge in. They would sit down together, dressed in their shawls, sipping a medium of porter, connishuring about matters that interested them, husbands, sons, daughters, babies, and perhaps giving the neighbours an odd lash of their tongues. Then the little Colman's Mustard tin which they all used as a snuff-box was produced from underneath the shawl and handed around, and every pinch taken was accompanied by a prayer. They never bought a drink for themselves, not because they were mean but because traditionally it was bought by their menfolk who then passed it to them through the hatch. The amount of drink that they consumed was minimal.

A story is told of a couple who lived in Gurranebraher. It was Christmas time and the wife decided to buy her husband a present of an O'Gorman cap. These caps, beloved of Corkmen and known as 'spoggers', were manufactured by the old Cork firm of O'Gormans whose factory was situated up near Shandon Steeple. It was customary for the men to go out on Christmas Eve, meet their friends and go drinking in various pubs. Anyhow this fellow decided to help maintain the long-observed tradition and as he was leaving the house his wife presented him with the new cap. He went off highly pleased with himself because an O'Gorman cap in those days was a prized possession, a status symbol of the highest order. He was well-oiled by the time he headed for home late that night, and as he was stumbling up along Cathedral Road he met a butty standing at an open door. The butty informed him that there was a party on inside and he was welcome to go in. Our friend did not need to be invited a second time. He knew that there would be no shortage of drink nor indeed of food there. In he went. Needless to say he enjoyed himself immensely. However, when he got home in the early hours of Christmas Morning who was waiting for him inside the door but the wife! That sobered him up fast.

'Where's your new cap?' she said in a no nonsense tone.

He put his hand to his head. Sure enough there was no cap

146

there. Then with an aplomb born of years of experience in such tight corners he tried to reassure her: 'Don't worry, Mary. Don't worry at all, girl. I know where it is.'

'How could you know where it is and you stotious coming home here to me? Is it codding me you are?'

'Honestly, girl, I know where it is all right. I left it in a house down in Cathedral Road. 'Twill be easy to find the house because they have a lovely gold toilet bowl.'

A gold toilet bowl in a house in Cathedral Road! He must be much worse than he appeared, she thought. However she was prepared to give him the benefit of the doubt.

'Go back down fast for it and remember you're not coming in here again until you get it.'

He turned around and meekly went out the door. He had a reasonably good idea where the house was and knocked on a door which he thought he recognised. A woman answered: 'Do you mind me asking you, Ma'am,' he says, 'but have ye a gold toilet bowl here in yeer house?'

She never answered him but turned around and shouted in to her own fellow in the backroom: 'Johnny, here's back the fella that done his pooley in your trumpet.'

He got back his cap because she was an understanding woman and knew that a man could pick up an old second-hand trumpet in any pawnshop any day, but to get a new O'Gorman cap and lose it was an unmitigated tragedy.

Some of the self-styled emancipated women of today seem to hold the view, and hold it ever so strongly, that married women of my generation and also of my mother's generation were the downtrodden chattels of their husbands, but with regard to most of the women with whom I was acquainted I can truthfully say that it is a mistaken view. Even when lack of money made life difficult there was a great bond between husband and wife. Neither would ever allow a third party to criticise the other and if they had a serious difference of opinion or even an argument they never mentioned or discussed it outside the home. They were only human and a row might erupt occasionally. The husband might lose his temper and give his wife a few pokes, but honestly I am not aware of any instance where a man seriously injured his wife. If there was any danger of that occurring the remedy was close at hand in the person of Fr O'Toole, a curate in our own Lough Parish. Fr O'Toole was a man of massive proportions and possessed a wonderful singing voice which thrilled the people of Cork each year on the occasion of the Corpus Christi procession. He could be harsh at times but he was an extremely fair-minded and caring man who could not abide injustice. If a man ill-treated his wife Fr O'Toole was sent for. He would call to the house at the earliest opportunity and, to put it at its mildest, by the time the priest's visit was over the errant husband had learned a salutary lesson. No man would ever strike a priest for it was firmly believed that if he did misfortune would dog him all the rest of his life, and even if he felt like doing so he wouldn't stand a chance against Fr O'Toole.

There was a tarry old man who once was very nasty to a young girl from the locality, so a few local men hauled him from his house and in front of everybody dragged him up Brandy Lane and Lough Road into the presbytery to let Fr O'Toole deal with him. By the time he emerged the 'taspee' had been well and truly knocked out of him and he was left with no desire to offend again.

People today might be horrified by such stories and some would quote them as support for their belief that we were a priest-ridden people. Be that as it may the system worked and was generally considered a remedy preferable to lawsuits and the sending of offenders to jail. After all the family of the culprit suffered as much as he himself did. As the women of the Northside used to remark: 'It is far better to be the mother of the wronged than to be the mother of the wrongdoer.'

Fr O'Toole was a blunt man who called a spade a spade and left nobody in doubt as to where he stood. In the early 1930s a daughter was born to a couple who lived in Gilabbey Street. Shortly before that Amelia Earhart had flown the Atlantic and this couple, like many other Irish people, acclaimed her feat. They held her in such high esteem that they wished their newborn to be named after her. When the father and the two gossips – they were the godparents – arrived at the Lough Church they informed Fr O'Toole of their wish, but he was having none of it and told them so. They stood their ground, however, and said that they would take the child to be baptised down in St Barrie's, the name by which the Protestant Cathedral was known to everybody in the area. Fr O'Toole retorted by saying that they were perfectly free to do so. A rumpus ensued with neither side prepared to yield so the child was returned unbaptised to her mother. A few days afterwards she was brought back to Fr O'Toole, this time with a different godfather. He baptised her, gave her the name of one of our Irish saints, and peace was restored.

Families dreaded the all too frequent slackage periods because unemployment threw them back so much in life and the dole money was not sufficient to enable them to get by until better times came. Having no financial resources they were compelled to go into debt. The pawnshops, infamous though these institutions are in some people's minds, were of great help to families in distress because they gave out money on clothing, jewellery and household goods. Some members of the community were filled with embarrassment any time they had to resort to pawning goods and they would walk up and down outside the shop waiting for the moment when nobody was around and they could dash in unseen. For others it was normal weekly routine.

Only men, known as clerks, worked in the pawnshops. This I always found rather strange because the mother of a family was always the person who did the pawning. Perhaps that was the way the women preferred it. These clerks were trained in assessing the value of jewellery and all other pawnable goods. The system was that when a woman pawned an article she got a certain amount of money against it as well as a ticket stating the amount to be paid back each week and also guaranteeing that the article in question would not be sold for six months. The owner could redeem the article at any time during that period by paying back the original amount together with whatever interest would have accrued. If this stipulation was not complied with the pawnbroker was then free to sell the article although in fairness it must be said that pawnbrokers were usually agreeable to extending the withholding period from six months to twelve provided the owner paid the extra interest.

Usually the first item a wife pawned was her husband's suit as normally it was required once a week at most for Sunday Mass. Her husband being unemployed was most unlikely to need it for any occasion or celebration. Sometimes she might pawn the suit unknown to him and in such a situation if he happened to need it and found it was missing there could indeed be a problem! Some pawnbrokers' clerks displayed great humanity. If a man's Sunday suit was in pawn then, provided the interest had been paid up, the clerk in deference to the wife's pleadings might agree to handing her over the suit on the Saturday evening, without any extra payment, on condition that she returned it again on the following Monday morning. In that way the husband could avoid the embarrassment of not being able to attend Sunday Mass. In some houses articles other than clothes were liable to disappear one by one, the mantel clock, perhaps, statues, bedclothes, fishing rods and the father's working tools. One woman of our acquaintance used to put her statue of St Anthony under her shawl and pawn it every Monday morning. On receiving her pension on the following Friday she would immediately return to the pawnshop and redeem St Anthony. The last thing of all to be pawned was the woman's wedding ring, and that occurred only when she was in dire circumstances such as the children being sick and in need of nourishment. If it was a twenty-two carat thick gold band she could expect to have thirty shillings advanced to her. Having received the money and prior to emerging from the pawn she would slip on her finger a brass ring

150

which she had already bought in Woolworth's for twopence as camouflage so that none of the neighbours would be any the wiser as to her financial predicament. She would then scrimp and save every penny she could, denying herself all comforts until she could redeem her wedding ring. Sadly some women were unable to do so and thus lost forever their most prized possession.

One day, not too long ago, I was standing at my door 'connishuring' with an older woman when an acquaintance of hers passed by without giving us a reck.

'Do you see that wan now?' says the old woman. 'She's out of her knowledge. She didn't even salute me and you wouldn't mind but my mother sometimes had to lend her mother my father's suit for the pawn because her father would take the living life out of her mother if she pawned his own one.'

On rare occasions younger men were known to avail of the facilities of the pawnshops. They were usually avid followers of the Cork hurling team, and would pawn their watches to enable them to make the fare to matches in Thurles, Limerick and even Croke Park. That was a measure of their devotion to the game.

The pawnbroking business was very brisk in those days. There was one pawnshop in Gilabbey Street, one on Sullivan's Quay and two in Barrack Street. One of the latter two, Finnegan's, was a fine shop with a large plate-glass window which displayed the articles not redeemed by their owners and consequently on open sale to the public. These included new blankets, sheets, shoes, shirts, and dresses. There was also a great array of jewellery, wedding and engagement rings, signet rings, emerald rings, sapphire rings, all displayed on a silver salver. Watches for both sexes filled another salver, and glass shelves in the window carried the clocks and vases which once had adorned sideboards and mantelpieces of people who had fallen on hard times.

Women in desperate financial straits who didn't have sufficient pawnable goods to raise the money they required could go to an order agent and take out orders. An order for perhaps five pounds might be taken out for a certain shop, maybe one of the largest in the city, and the holder could then go to that shop and buy goods to the value of five pounds. The agent would then call to the woman's home every Friday night to collect the agreed five shillings per week over a period not of twenty weeks but of twenty-four. The extra four weeks' instalment represented the agent's profit. Taking out orders was the most commonly used means of dressing children for their First Communion and Confirmation. Sometimes mothers in desperation would get an order and go to a shop to purchase new sheets and blankets which they would promptly pawn. Very often they were unable to redeem these articles and that is how the pawnbroker came to have unused goods for sale in his shop.

Moneylenders were another group to whom women had recourse when in difficulties. These moneylenders charged interest at the rate of four shillings for every pound. Should a woman borrow five pounds she received only four, the other pound being retained as immediate interest, yet she was required to pay an agreed weekly sum until the five pounds were repaid. If later on the unfortunate woman was still in financial difficulties and could not comply with the conditions she pleaded with the moneylender to grant her a second loan before the first had been cleared. Soon she found herself deeper and deeper in debt. What such poor creatures wouldn't give for a credit union!

It was customary for loan offices to give loans only to women whose husbands were in regular employment. Molly O', whom I knew well, required a loan very urgently, but unfortunately her husband was out of work. She decided to bring him with her to the loan office in the hope that he might bolster up her courage, but she wasn't too confident of success. They spent a few minutes walking up and down the street outside the office trying to work out the best way of handling the moneylender. Suddenly Molly espied a bus conductor in uniform on his way to work. Dashing over to him she whipped the cap off the head of the unsuspecting conductor saying: 'One minute there now, boy, and I'll give yeh back yer cap again.' She rushed back to her husband, rammed the cap down on his head and marshalled him in the door to the moneylender who, on seeing her spouse complete with the official headgear, decided that there was no need to ask the dreaded question: 'Is himself in employment?' Molly got her loan and the astonished busman had his cap returned to him within minutes. That woman who could scarcely write her name had outwitted a man with a first-class education and proven business acumen, thus confirming St Finbarr's prophecy that Cork would never rear a fool.

More Interesting Books

MAURA'S BOY

A CORK CHILDHOOD

CHRISTY KENNEALLY

Maura's Boy describes the first ten years of the life of Christy
Kenneally, a working-class Cork northsider who lost his
mother when he was five years of age. The book captures with
remarkable effect that sorrow and the compensating love
given by his father, Dave, his grandparents and a regiment of
aunts, uncles and cousins. The life is a simple one yet full of the
adventures provided by the Lane and Quarry and the other
places in the wonderland that formed the landscape of his
childhood. The account of the changing seasons in the streets,
the green places, churches, sportsgrounds, seaside resorts is
magical as is the delineation of the relatives, neighbours,
priests and teachers whose wisdom, humour and love re-
created the boy who might otherwise have slumped into
misery. The picture of the city, with the lightly expressed but
fundamental schism between northside and southside, is a
piece of closely observed social history of the time (1948–58)
when the city had near full employment and hurling and films
were the pre-occupation of its youth. The book is as much
about the place as the narrator, and beautifully conveys the
sense of a lost golden age.

THE DAYS OF THE SERVANT BOY

LIAM O'DONNELL

'A day of great importance' – so Liam O'Donnell describes the time of the yearly hiring fair. A well-known feature of Irish farming life in his youth, it seems now a throwback to the distant past.

Though Liam O'Donnell's account of the days of the servant boy deals with the practice in County Cork the basic idea was the same throughout the country: the bonding of labouring men and women to farmers for a fixed term at a 'paltry' rate.

The author as a farmer's son was in an ideal position to describe the lives these hirelings had to lead with long hours, back-breaking work and often primitive living conditions.

His account is lively, often funny – for the story was not all gloom – and the reader is presented with an unforgettable picture of one of our Irish yesterdays, and left with the same great admiration that the author feels for the people he portrays so well.

THE TAILOR AND ANSTY

ERIC CROSS

''Tis a funny state of affairs when you think of it'. It is the tailor himself speaking. *'This book is nothing but the fun and the talk and the laughter which has gone on for years around this fireside ...'*

The Tailor and Ansty was banned soon after its first publication in 1942 and was the subject of such bitter controversy that it may well have influenced the later relaxation of the censorship law. Certainly it has become a modern Irish classic, promising to make immortals of the Tailor and his irrepressible foil, his wife, Ansty, and securing a niche in Irish letters for their Boswell, Eric Cross.

The Tailor never travelled further than Scotland and yet the width of the world can hardly contain his wealth of humour and fantasy. Marriages, inquests, matchmaking, wakes – everything is here. Let the Tailor round it off with a verse of a ballad:

Now all you young maidens,
Don't listen to me
For I will incite you to immortalitee,
Or unnatural vice or in a similar way
Corrupt or deprave you or lead you astray.

THE APPRENTICE

ÉAMON KELLY

The Apprentice is the autobiography of the actor and seanchaí (storyteller) Éamon Kelly. It takes its title from the time when young Kelly was apprenticed to his father, a wheelwright and master craftsman. The book lovingly recreates an area – the Sliabh Luachra region east of Killarney – a family life and a culture that co-existed with dramatic political events: the First World War, the War of Independence and the Civil War. It also provides a unique glimpse into the mind and emotions of a gifted artist as he grew to maturity. Funny, sad, informative and moving by turns, *The Apprentice* has an appeal for several generations of readers.

THE MAN FROM CAPE CLEAR
A TRANSLATION BY RIOBÁRD P. BREATNACH OF
CONCHÚR Ó SÍOCHÁIN'S SEANCHAS CHLÉIRE

Conchúr Ó Síocháin lived all his days on Cape Clear island, the southern outpost of an old and deep-rooted civilisation. He lived as a farmer and a fisherman and his story vividly portrays life on that island which has Fastnet Rock as its nearest neighbour. He was a gifted storyteller, a craftsman and a discerning folklorist. Here he tells of life on the island drawing on the ancient traditions and the tales handed down from the dim past. There is a sense of humour, precision and a great sense of community on every page.

The Man from Cape Clear is a collection of memories and musings, topography and tales, and contains a fund of seafaring yarns not to be found elsewhere. It discloses aspects of insular life which should delight the inner eye of the world at large and enrich every Irishman's grasp of his heritage.

Ó Síocháin died in February 1941 and is buried beside Teampall Chiaráin on the island.

LETTERS FROM IRISH COLLEGE

EDITED BY ROSE DOYLE

Do you remember being in Irish college in Spiddal, Ring, Muiríoch or Gortahork? Or your children leaving home alone for the first time and going west or south?

Irish college is a unique rite of passage for Irish adolescents. It is where they first experience homesickness, friendships they may keep for life, first love, the value of money and the great crack of céilís.

This collection, which spans the years 1936 to 1995, includes several letters from Ring in County Waterford written in Irish and English by former Taoiseach Garret FitzGerald. And dozens more from people, famous and not so famous, from all walks of Irish life.

MÉINÍ
THE BLASKET NURSE

LESLIE MATSON

This is the life story of a remarkable woman, Méiní Dunlevy. Born in Massachusetts of Kerry parents, Méiní was reared in her grandparents' house in Dunquin. When she was nineteen, she eloped with an island widower to the Great Blasket, where she worked as a nurse and midwife for thirty-six years. Returning widowed to Dunquin, she died in 1967, aged 91.

Méiní's story, recorded by the author from her own accounts and those of her friends and relatives in Dunquin, is an evocation of a forceful, spicy personality and a compelling reconstruction of a way of life that has exercised an enduring fascination for readers. *Méiní, the Blasket Nurse* is a worthy successor to *An t-Oileánach* and *Twenty Years a-Growing*.

LETTERS FROM THE GREAT BLASKET

Eibhlís Ní Shúilleabháin

This selection of *Letters from the Great Blasket*, for the most part written by Eibhlís Ní Shúilleabháin of the island to George Chambers in London, covers a period of over twenty years. Eibhlís married Seán Ó Criomhthain – a son of Tomás, An tOileánach (The Islandman). On her marriage she lived in the same house as the Islandman and nursed him during the last years of his life which are described in the letters. Incidentally, the collection includes what must be an unique specimen of the Islandman's writing in English in the form of a letter expressing his goodwill towards Chambers.

Beginning in 1931 when the island was still a place where one might marry and raise a family (if only for certain exile in America) the letters end in 1951 with the author herself in exile on the mainland and 'the old folk of the island scattering to their graves'. By the time Eibhlís left the Blasket in July 1942 the island school had already closed and the three remaining pupils 'left to run wild with the rabbits'.

FAVOURITE POEMS WE LEARNED IN SCHOOL

Chosen and Introduced by
THOMAS F. WALSH

Thomas F. Walsh has put together a collection of the most quoted and most memorable poems we learned in school. The poems in this anthology will remain with us until we reach the end of our journey in this life, mainly because we learned them when we were young, and consequently they have become part of us.

The poems are evocative and they will stir a nostalgic chord in all our hearts.

FAVOURITE POEMS WE LEARNED IN SCHOOL AS GAEILGE

Chosen and Introduced by
THOMAS F. WALSH

In this volume Thomas F. Walsh has collected together some of the most popular and memorable poems in Irish that we all learned in school. These are poems containing lines, words, sounds that go round and round in our heads years after we think we have forgotten them.

This book gives the reader the opportunity to savour again the treasures of our youth. They are poems we want to read, rather than the poems we have to read.